MUD, SNOW, AND CYCLOCROSS

HOW 'CROSS TOOK OVER US CYCLING

MUD, SNOW, AND CYCLOCROSS
HOW 'CROSS TOOK OVER US CYCLING

MOLLY HURFORD

Deeds Publishing | Atlanta

Published in the United States of America

Published by Deeds Publishing, Marietta, GA

www.deedspublishing.com

Library of Congress Cataloging-in-Publications Data is available upon request.

ISBN 978-1-937565-35-0

Books are available in quantity for promotional or premium use. For information, write Deeds Publishing, PO Box 682212, Marietta, GA 30068 or info@deedspublishing.com.

First Edition, 2012

10 9 8 7 6 5 4 3 2

CONTENTS

DEDICATION

To the Rutgers Cycling crew, because without them, I never would have started this craziness, or ended up with a cowbell tattoo.

My Parents, for being endlessly supportive and schlepping to (and pitting at) countless races.

New England & Mid Atlantic scene, because the people I've met through cyclocross haven't just become race buddies, they've become friends, housemates, neighbors and so, so much more.

And, of course, everyone who submitted willingly to interview after interview with me!

FOREWORD

I've been in love with cyclocross since my first race, which I remember in great, great detail. I'd been peer pressured into trying a cyclocross race because my team at the time, Rutgers University Cycling, needed women's points in order to preserve their dominance of the Eastern Collegiate Cycling Conference. So, on a borrowed bike in pouring rain, I did my first race at Granogue in Delaware. And despite the fact that I got last, or maybe second to last, in the Women's 3/4 field, I was hooked.

Maybe it was the childlike fun of playing in the mud. Maybe it was the sense of belonging. Maybe it was the fun that Charlie, Pat, Mark, Matt and I had in the van driving to and from races. Heck, maybe it was the skinsuits. Whatever the reason, cyclocross quickly took over my life.

I'm happy to say that I helped the team preserve their winning streak that year. The trophy for winning the overall conference? A giant cowbell. When we kept the title again the next year, and I started developing some level of competence—like learning how to remount halfway through the season—the five of us decided to get matching cowbell tattoos. It was late and we were tired and coming home from a race. But we did it, because that's what cyclocross does to people.

The next year, my old teammate and close friend, Blake, got me onto the team he was managing, Rockstar Games/Signature Cycles. I was worried that cyclocross wouldn't be the same after college, since I wouldn't be with my group of close friends any more. I couldn't have been more wrong, because I met some of the greatest people in the world that season. I also started working for *Cyclocross Magazine,* primarily (I believe) due to the fact that I had the cowbell tattoo. Being able to work in cyclocross meant talking to my idols—I was nearly speechless the first time I interviewed Tim Johnson, which made for an awkward phone interview—and got to spend time with great people like Adam Myerson and the whole Keough family, all under the guise of being at work. When work is also your passion, you're the luckiest person in the world.

So when the chance to write the book on cyclocross in the US came up, I couldn't have been more excited. Not just because I was writing a book, but because these people I've interviewed deserve to be recognized for their amazing talents.

Be forewarned, this book is an oral history, a reflection on cyclocross in the past 40 years in the US. It isn't by any means comprehensive, complete, or finished. There are plenty of racers, past and present, that aren't included, because to add every single person in is simply impossible. Rather, this is a series of snapshots of cyclocross in America in the last four decades that come together to form an album that chronicles the development and hints at the future. I hope it's as enjoyable reading it as it was interviewing so many amazing people and writing it all down.

This is US 'Cross.

© Dejan Smaic

1: WHAT IS CYCLOCROSS?

"Cyclocross is a far more emotional cycling event than anything else. I think it's because you're on the limit right from the beginning. It has more tragedy—mechanical tragedy, crashes, rolled tires—it's a game of mistakes, it's very much like a Shakespearean drama."

–Richard Fries

The day was frigid. The first snow of the season had just graced New England, blanketing the course with powder and creating conditions that turned racers nearly hypothermic as they raced around the course, putting out extra wattage to increase circulation. It was the last race of the season for many of us, NBX Grand Prix of Cyclocross in Warwick, Rhode Island. The battle for the series win had come down to this last race, these last five minutes of the elite men's race. Cyclocross legend Adam Myerson was battling for the lead with one of New England's native cyclocross sons, Nick Keough. Behind him, Justin Lindine, Myerson's competitor for the series title, blazed around the course, furiously nipping at the two leaders' heels. As they flew smoothly through the barriers, the crowd of spectators screamed and cheered, ablaze with a freshly remembered love of the sport, the realization that the season was coming to an end and we'd all go our separate ways with our separate lives for the next eight months. The finish line was under a stone bridge that overlooked the course, less than a mile from the barriers. The crowd, divided on who they wanted the winner to be but happy just to be there, let out a deafening roar.

Like one fluid mass, the group turned and ran towards the bridge overlooking the finish, and quieted as we watched the men round the last few corners. Keough crossed the line inches ahead, taking the win, but for Myerson, the win of the race itself wasn't what mattered. And later, at the awards ceremony, as his eyes filled with tears as he took the medal for winning the overall Verge series that he had started, that he had organized, that he had raced, that he had won, we knew that we were all part of something special. As he raised his arms in victory on the podium, we all won. We were part of a sport that, in becoming involved with it, had changed our lives.

A year later, I was in Madison, Wisconsin, watching the elite men once again battle it out for the National title. With one lap to go, Jeremy Powers flew off the front of the five-man breakaway, struggling to take the one win that had eluded him the past few years. He'd narrowly missed out on the win thanks to crashes, mechanicals, or just not being "on" at the right second. And this year, he was poised for victory. The crowds, again, went wild. The spectators were mainly racers who were tired, bruised, cold and ready to party.

No matter what racer you were rooting for when the race began, when Jeremy Powers crossed that finish line in first place, one hand in the air, the other covering his face, your heart filled up. When Powers rolled into his fiancé's arms and the two hugged and cried and he shook his head and said, "Finally," every reporter in the vicinity choked back tears.

These are the moments.

There is poetry in cycling. A certain grace, a fluidity, a ballet. Pedals smoothly turning over, taking a corner in the perfect apex, casually dipping so close to the asphalt that you can almost touch the gravel with your cheek.

Then, there's cyclocross. Grace and fluidity are in short supply as even the most elite riders fumble through mud pits, focusing not on expediency of motion, but merely staying upright. And yes, there's a type of poetry in bunny-hopping the barriers with perfect, precision timing. But those moments, undefinable in their strange beauty, are surrounded by loud, harsh movements, cold mud and muck, sleet, snow and anything Mother Nature can throw at the men and women who strive for greatness. To watch cyclocross is to see cyclists at their most raw, burning every match and then using the matchsticks as kindling as the bell rings for the last lap. They charge the course, funneling into sharp turns and sandpits and barriers and steep climbs. And they're doing it directly in front of cheering crowds, splattering mud over the beer-swilling, screaming fans.

"It's a crazy cocktail of testosterone and adrenaline and endorphins," announcer Richard Fries says. "It's far more emotional announcing 'cross. In cyclocross, you have witnesses to everything that you do."

It's hard, but it's also fun. "You can be having the shittiest day on the bicycle and still be having a blast, taking hand ups and having fun," Raleigh Bicycles' Brian Fornes explains. "It's just pure encouragement from the crowd. Everyone sticks around and watches races and cheers. Your kids can hang out at it, you can take in the entire race, it's something you can't do with any other race. It's as personal as you can get to the pros out there."

How do you explain cyclocross to a person who's never seen a race? Go to your computer, Google cyclocross, click on a video clip, watch it, and then come back. Got it? Good. Now keep reading.

Showing is the easiest way to explain cyclocross, since even the pros have a tough time with the question. Take Tim Johnson, one of the top elite racers in the US, who's been racing cyclocross for nearly twenty years. "I have such a hard time with it. To anyone active, it's like a cross-country running race, but we do it on bikes. People automatically get a picture of that in their minds. But then I say we're racing as fast as we possibly can and it's really intense and people fly out of corners and then crash, all that stuff … it makes it hard to explain."

In fact, he thinks that the lack of an accurate, simple description is what keeps cyclocross a more underground genre of cycling. "This is the real problem for our sport. There's such a hook with our sport when as soon as people get close to it, they totally get hooked and get into it. But there's not a big, wide explanation that people might consider looking into it on their own. It's like we're a flytrap with no smell. You're stuck if you happen to land on it."

"A flytrap with no smell" might be the most perfect description of cyclocross ever uttered, because it's oddly accurate. Cyclocross is not a sport that sounds like fun: racing in mud, carrying bikes up steep hills, trudging along in sand, sliding out in dusty corners, strange bruises cropping up in bizarre places. Most people, upon hearing you describe it, would wonder why you'd ever choose, week in and week out, to subject yourself to that kind of torture and pay for the pleasure of doing it. But do one race, or be a spectator at one race, and suddenly, you're hooked. If you happen to come across a race, whether through friends or just because you happen to pass by a course set up in a local park, that's where the flytrap effect happens, and you're caught.

Veteran cyclocrosser Pete Webber poetically describes a cyclocross bike by saying, "A 'cross bike is difficult to ride in rough terrain — but harder is better in cross, that is why it is a cult sport. Picture yourself smokin' into the first turn of a race, sketched out in a two-wheel drift, shoulder-to-shoulder with a pack of crazies—it's just not the same on a fat-tire mountain bike." Still not convinced? Keep reading.

American racer and world legend Katie Compton has a simpler explanation, though even the simplest of explanations of cyclocross requires the use of a metaphor: "It's like a cross between mountain and road racing. I usually say the bike is kind of like the SUV of bikes, you can ride it on road or off road. It's fun on the road, it's fun on the dirt, but it's not your four-wheel drive vehicle."

And unlike road racing, tactics aren't as key, and racing is hard and fast from the gun. Elite racer Amy Dombroski says, "You put everything out there in that 40 minutes and then you're done. I like just going as hard as I can, but for a short period of time." And the other half of the equation is what happens after the race is over, Dombroski explains. "Then, you can drink beer and eat yummy things when you're done with it. And the people who race, they're just great personalities and a wonderful community of people. It's a lot more laid back but at the same time, everyone's out there giving it their all."

In fact, racing cyclocross is akin to what kids do every single day on their bikes. When Andrew Yee, the founder of *Cyclocross Magazine*, talks about discovering cyclocross, he says, "It seemed exactly like my kind of riding. As a kid, I did that kind of riding in the woods and fields behind my parent's house."

Cyclocross in the United States is different than anywhere else in the world. In Europe, cyclocross racing happens at the elite level, and races are attended much like football games: there, crowds 20,000 deep pay for the privilege of watching their favorite pros compete. Racers are rock stars, residing in trailers with their names and faces emblazoned on the outside. *Cyclocross Magazine* reporter Kat Statman points out, "We don't treat racers with as much celebrity status as they do in Europe. If you read *Sporza* and look at what they write about Euro cyclocrossers, it's like reading the *National Enquirer.*"

Katie Compton laid out the key differences in the races between Europe and the US, and for her, it's not the crowds or the atmosphere. As a racer, she notices the ground under her knobby tires before all of that. "I think the major difference is the technical aspect of the courses. They're just laid out differently, they're created for the pros. There is always a technical 'oh shit' factor in the races. They're courses where you can't pedal around the turns. If they're not heavy and muddy, they make them fast and technical. There are tricky on and off the bike sections. The competition is just stiffer. The Belgians are starting to pay attention to the women's racing too, and it's kind of growing and getting more entertaining."

"It's evolved differently, just in the sheer wildfire grassroots growth we've had," Jonny "El Gato" Sundt explains. "And the experience of what American 'cross is from the competition to the drinking beer to the heckling to the hanging out with your friends, it's really phenomenal. And it's often overlooked."

And over the years, cyclocross has grown in the US but stayed true to its original character: serious races, fun atmosphere, grassroots organization. "It's grown in many ways but it's stayed the same in many ways. In the US, the number of participants has grown substantially, there's more support and more races," Stu Thorne, the founder of CyclocrossWorld. com, says. "But it's still similar in that it's still a core group of people, it's a lot of the same people that were involved. Guys like Adam Myerson, Tom Stevens, Paul Curley. We used to race around for a trophy that Tom made in his garage, where he'd take a ribbon and an old 17 tooth cog off of a freewheel, maybe polish it up, and staple it together. And the placing was written in magic marker on the ribbon. There was very little money involved."

In the US, because cyclocross is more participant-based as opposed to spectator-based, courses tend to be missing that "factor" mentioned by Compton. The courses, while technical in many ways, often lack the real technical difficulty provided by Euro courses. While this may be good for developing the sport for amateur riders, the American promoters are at a crossroads: the decision needs to be made in coming years which direction they wish to see cyclocross develop. If it's a participant sport with an elite field, the courses will remain the same. But if the US wants to develop a truly elite field that has a chance at competing against the well-paid Euro riders, courses need to get more technical, and riders need to be challenged more.

Right now, however, even the governing body of cycling in the US believes that cyclocross is right where it needs to be in the US. Marc Gullickson of USA Cycling says it's a great sport in this country because, "It's accessible to the fans, and it's nice to see our top racers put aside time to talk to the fans and be available. The top 'cross racers are, in their own right, quite popular cyclists in the US. Take Jeremy Powers, with his online reality show based around 'cross. He's excited about incoming talent and he'll talk to them."

This excitement is contagious, and rarely do you find a racer who doesn't have incredibly strong feelings about the sport. It's never a job, it's always a passion, from the highest to the lowest level of riders. Even race promoters who've spent their lives putting on major road races are charmed immediately when they attend cyclocross races, and can see a big future because of the passion that racers and spectators put into it. Joan Hanscom of the United States Gran Prix (USGP) series says, "It's so TV friendly, and media friendly. Right away I knew it was exciting stuff. I thought it was really cool watching people running around and ringing cowbells."

The most poignant part of cyclocross in the United States is perhaps the rider's own views of what's important, and that's what makes it so unique and so beautiful. When I interviewed Kaitie Antonneau and asked her what her favorite moment in cyclocross has been, I assumed she'd say finishing second at Nationals. Instead, she replied, "It wasn't racing. Probably right after I crossed the finish line at Nationals and hugged Katie [Compton]. That's my best moment, and I think that will be my best moment for a long time. And you're just happy. There's nothing else in the world that can wreck the moment. It's perfect."

Those are the moments that we work for in this sport, and those are the moments that make cyclocross so unique as a sport. Elite Nationals is a perfect example: Jeremy Powers crossed the line to take his first National title, one hand covering his face as he cried from happiness and relief, hugging his now-fiancé, also crying. Those of us gathered around to write the race reports all found ourselves choked up, watching the tableau. Just an hour before, Katie Compton had taken the women's win, and Kaitie Antonneau had come in, crying and smiling and hugging Compton, and then Nicole Duke, her teammate who rolled in seconds behind. Instead of each rider taking his or her podium spot or rolling to their respective tents or vehicles, riders lingered in the finishing area, high fiving, hugging, and—even if the race didn't go the way they would have hoped—genuinely congratulating the other winners.

It sounds cliché, but racing cyclocross in the US is akin to having a massive extended family: there's laughter, tears, happiness, the occasional dramatic moment, surprises, and so much love shared based on this common bond. And granted, that bond involves spending weekends getting covered in mud, shivering with borderline hypothermia, and pushing our legs as far as they can be pushed. But in its own way, it's beautiful.

© Pedal Power Photography

This is a defining moment for cyclocross in the States. With the World Championships finally coming to the US in 2013, the level of racing among the elite racers will be raised substantially, and with cyclocross as the fastest growing cycling discipline in the US, according to USA Cycling, it stands to reason that it will continue to grow among the amateur ranks as well. "The sky is the limit as bike racing grows," racer, promoter and team manager Adam Myerson says. "I think what you're seeing now is that numbers for road and mountain are growing because people who race 'cross are looking for ways to stay fit in the summer. Who expected that 'cross was going to be the gateway to road or mountain biking as opposed to the other way around? The fact that that's happening says to me that we're not close to the top."

What started out as a way for roadies to keep fit in the fall by playing in nearby parks and fields has turned legitimate. "I think it's going to be a huge season because of Worlds, everyone's going to be paying attention to it, and all the people who've been thinking about doing 'cross are going to pay attention this year," Myerson continues. "This year and the year after, there will be a continued effect from Worlds. I think those seasons will be record-breaking everywhere."

And what happens after a race? Richard Fries puts it simply, "15 minutes after you've gone through this emotionally draining experience, you're hanging out, drinking a beer. I love that about cyclocross."

© Pedal Power Photography

THE PROS WEIGH IN ON HOW TO DESCRIBE CROSS

© Pedal Power Photography

"It's a bike race that generally happens in city parks on varied terrain and it's fast. A mountain bike would be too slow. If you're explaining it to someone who doesn't race bikes, it's like 'Hey, I want you to listen very carefully while I explain this, because it's going to sound really dumb. But it's awesome.' Or, 'I'm about to tell you about something that's going to make absolutely no sense. And in fact, the more I tell you about it, I wonder why I even do it.' Honestly, if you do a proper job of explaining what cyclocross is to someone who doesn't know, you should, by the end of the explanation, question why you race 'cross." —Jonny "El Gato" Sundt

"I struggle with this one, it's so hard! You ride off-road, it's not mountain biking, you have to get off and run over things. I get so uncomfortable trying to describe it! A lot of people I describe it to don't like it because you have to get off your bike." —Kaitlin Antonneau

I would describe it as very similar to an arena sport where you're able to watch a lot of it from one point. It's very fast, exciting, and fun racing to watch. It's not like any other form of cycling. You can understand it just by watching, the first person is the winner and the strongest person wins. For someone who hasn't seen it, I think it'd be great to grab a beer or other beverage, a nice tall lemonade, sit back and take in the energy and excitement that one of the races bring, and watch people suffer. If you like sports, it's something great and physically demanding, and technically demanding as well. It's got a lot of things that mountain biking and road racing don't have, in that they're hard to follow because you can't see it. In cyclocross, everything is out there, every single move can get scrutinized.   –Jeremy Powers

I always just tell people, it's like road racing. But it's off-road. But it's not mountain biking. And we run. Usually I just pull out my phone and pull up a video of a World Cup or something. I've never said it's a steeplechase or anything.   –Molly Cameron

"A race on bikes not designed to be doing what we're doing on them. That's the fun part of it, I think. It's crazy, especially when it gets muddy."
                                                            –Geoff Kabush

"You take a road bike. You put knobby tires on it. You're racing on a short course, like a crit but a bit longer, and usually there's some road, there might be mud, grass, sand, gravel, or a hill where you have to get off and run. It challenges your aerobic and anaerobic systems and also your ability to handle your bike, your ability to get on and off the bike. It's a series of shifting terrains with varying degrees of difficulty."   –Mark Vareschi

"I tend to tell them it's like a schoolyard with a mile circuit around it, on the grass, on the pavement, and picking the bike up and putting it on your shoulder and running up the hills, over hurdles."   –Jonathan Page

"A lot of people say that it is like steeplechase but with bikes, and that is pretty accurate. But I like to say it is like motocross without the motors. Other types of bike racing are not as much fun as cyclocross. It is hard to describe exactly why, however. I think it's a combination of things. 'Cross is grassroots and low key. It is about family, the people, the culture. The races are short and tight, the competition is always close, and there aren't many racers on the course. It's fast and intense and always exciting. Plus, the season is short and well-defined—only a few months separate the first and last race in the schedule, so your energy is always high."

                      –Pete Webber

"I run into this problem a lot. I usually go for: you ride a road bike with knobby tires and it's a combination of road and mountain biking. It always throws people for a loop. They can kind of picture it but until you get out there it's hard to understand what it's all about. You ride around a field and jump on and off your bike and it sounds ridiculous. Then you get out there and do it, and it's fun."

                      –Luke Keough

"Take a road bike, put knobby tires on it, rip around the fields and hop over barriers. Most people don't get it anyway and that's OK. I appreciate that they care enough to ask what it is. I warn people, 'if you race it, everything else you do will seem stupid. It's harder. You can get better results on the road or other places. Come race 'cross, you'll get your ass kicked but you won't want to race anything else.'" –Fat Marc

"It's one of those things you just have to see to understand. It's like a road race and a mountain bike race combined, the best of the two combined. Like a road and mountain race but without the crappy parts."

                      –Ryan Trebon

"It's funny because I always have to describe it. People are always like, 'cyclo-what?' So I just say I'm on a road bike with knobby tires and we do a mile and a half loop, race for forty minutes and it's basically an all-out sprint. It's technical and it's challenging and it's in the elements. It's through mud, rain, sleet, everything. It's the tough man sport of the cycling world."   —Nicole Duke

"Road biking and mountain biking meets beer and cowbells."
—Colt McElwaine

"I just had to do this at a grocery store. I say it's a road bike with wider, more mountain-bike-style tires on a mostly off-road course with some pavement, and that's usually about where I leave it. Beyond that, any more detail and people just get confused, and then I get confused, and confuse them more."   —Zach McDonald

"I like the description: the steeplechase of cycling. It looks a lot easier than it is, that's for sure. The speed isn't very high when you're riding through soft grass compared to the speed of a road race but it requires constant power. It's like doing a crit without the drafting."
—Todd Wells

"I try to describe it as the equivalent of a cross country running race on a road bike with knobby tires. That usually gets the point across."
—Adam Myerson

"It's a road race with less traction."   —Mark McCormack

"I say that it's the steeplechase of cycling. A lot of people know running and know what steeplechase is, and that resonates with them. I usually say that it's a really asinine sport."   —Amy Dombroski

"I usually liken the effort to a 10k running race, in effort and duration. A lot of people are familiar with a 10k race or that effort of intensity, which is pretty hard from the gun. I say it's a three kilometer running course that's similar to a cross country running course. For me, that means it's not gnarly like a mountain bike course and it's not a lot of pavement. And for most people, that makes sense to them. And people love to see pictures of people carrying their bikes. That's an odd part of cycling, to not be on the bike, so I always include that in the description. When it's rainy and muddy and snowy, there's an element of the ridiculous, but I think that makes it more awesome."　　　　　　　　　　　—Mo Bruno Roy

"Steeplechase. But you're carrying the horse. Actually, cyclocross is like a night on the town in reverse. You start out almost blacking out and feeling like you're going to vomit. Then you start drinking."

—Bill Schieken

"It's a combination of Nascar and steeplechase. It's a short course: obstacles, dirt, pavement, grass, mud, on the bike, off the bike, and all really intense for an hour."　　　　　　　　　　—Joan Hanscom

"It bothers me when people try to describe it where it's so extreme or masochistic. That bothers me because it takes away the elegance of it. They make it sound like it's a Marine drill type thing, when I want them to realize how brilliant the riders are. When I think of steeplechase, I think of something that's elegant and fast. When you say you race 'cross, you're immediately vaulted into 'you're the the real deal.'"　　　—Richard Fries

"The bikes are different. Drop bars and thin tires, but with knobs so we can get traction off road ... There is no suspension, the bikes are rigid, light and fast both on- and off- road. The track is a short circuit which varies depending on available terrain of the park—there can be dirt, sand, pavement, gravel, mud, snow, etc. There usually are short running sections, which we carry the bike, often over barriers- natural or man made. So FUN to participate and watch!"　　　　-Mary McConneloug

"It combines road and mountain biking without the big tires, it puts a premium on technical skills like being able to remount and dismount on your bike. But I also tend to go into the more outlandish description, which is: what you see is what you get racing. The guy who's in the front is likely the guy who's going to win the race. It's an oversimplification, but it is different from road racing. It's in-your-face racing. You come out and see that 'this guy is going hard.' It's full gun racing, from the beginning." —Brook Watts

Racing on a typical US course — around a schoolyard — CyclocrossWorld.com owner Stu Thorne was one of the early adapters of the cyclocross bike.   Photo by Robin MacDonal-Foley

Note the skinny, slick road tires on cyclocross legend Don Myrah's early 90's cyclocross rig.   Photo by Robin MacDonal-Foley

2: A BRIEF HISTORY OF CYCLOCROSS

"I started with toe clips, soccer shoes, heavy touring bikes, and a hairnet helmet, no internet, 15 rider fields (this was everyone racing together—Juniors, Women, Masters, Elite). A lot has changed."
                                                              —Mark McCormack

Cyclocross in the United States has a long and varied history. The farthest back that people can recall it being a viable form of racing is the 1960s, and the first official National Championship was run in 1974. Arguably, that can be listed as the official starting date of cyclocross as a national sport, as opposed to a game racers played in fields in inclement weather to build fitness and skill for other disciplines.

Like all American history, where in the country you are makes all the difference. Kat Statman, one of the first *Cyclocross Magazine* reporters, says that, "There's a weird American history, and it's still this way: our regions are very split up in the ways that cyclocross exists. New England is not Portland, which is not the Midwest, which is not the Southeast." Cyclocross has developed differently in the various regions of the country, ranging from the development of a serious racing atmosphere to that of a wildly fun party scene centered around a few races. Additionally, there's been different degrees of development from the grassroots level of racing—local races with local racers that may or may not be sanctioned or officially scored—to a more professional quality of racing that brings in top level pro racers from around the country and world.

In the '70s, when cyclocross was a slow growing scene scattered throughout the country, it was simply a labor of love, a compulsion. "Aside from being a 'cross promoter, I'm a cross fanatic, and for three decades," Brook Watts says. "I've been riding my bike in order to get ready for 'cross season. I pine for 'cross season."

"Nationals were held in 1976 in Milwaukee," Watts remembers. "Then, we got the bright idea to bring Nationals to Austin. In fact, Nationals in 2015 will be at the exact same park. Criminals always return to the scene of the crime."

Legends Tom Stevens, Jason Snow, and Paul Curley on a snowy course in the early 90s   Photo by Robin MacDonal-Foley

"I got involved with 'cross racing when I was a student at the University of Texas. I raced in the fall of '76 and got my ass kicked. 13th out of 14 guys, I think," Watts fondly recalls. "Austin was the Boulder of the cycling world in the 1970s. Everyone went there to train in the winter. So I convinced my parents I was moving there for college, but really I moved there for the cycling, the 18-year-old liquor laws, the music scene, and because you could walk down the street and everyone was smoking pot. It was the 1970s, let's be honest. My life back then was very different than it is today."

Races were often held in school yards, and announcer Richard Fries fondly remembers standing on jungle gyms to announce the action. Here, a young Adam Myerson does some of his first racing in his long cyclocross career.
Photo by Robin MacDonal-Foley

Watts isn't the only one who fell in love with cyclocross instantly, even if he did so in an area not known for its impressive cyclocross scene.

New England, on the other hand, was an instant hotbed for cyclocross. One of the long time racers is New England's Paul Curley. He's been racing since cyclocross began growing in the US and is still one of the top racers in his Masters field. "I got into it after my first season of riding the road because I just loved the racing part of it," he says. "I came to bike racing from not being able to run, the track thing was over and shifted my energy to cycling. When the Fall came around, I was so bummed that there weren't more road races, and someone told me about cyclocross, so I decided to do that. I rode my road bike and it was basically just cones thrown around a field, and you rode around the course. There were never more than ten of us and it was pretty laid back."

These early races are remembered fondly by racers now, but most racers will agree that courses today are much better, and races are much more professional. Mo Bruno Roy recalls that, "Some of the races I saw were a blur. People were on mountain bikes, just riding around a sort-of course. The courses themselves weren't as developed and now the professionalism that is coming along even with smaller venues is really impressive."

However, by the 90s, race promoters were starting to understand the need to have solid, structured courses. The unofficial "Godfather of Cyclocross," Paul Curley, remembers, "I promoted Nationals in 1992 in Boston. The crew that marked the course was the group that ran the Mount Snow mountain bike race. I think that made a difference, when you start paying professionals to mark the course, then you have a more defined course, a more spectator friendly course. It's the first time we had pros and amateur fields, locker room facilities and hot showers, we charged admission, it took it to a slightly higher level."

But even though Nationals were a bigger deal, *Cyclocross Magazine's* Andrew Yee remembers that, "Nationals and the elite races really weren't any different than a local, grassroots race. They were pretty much one and the same, the only difference was a couple dozen people traveled across the country to attend Nationals, but it's not like you had fans and groupies and big parties at the races."

He adds, "There was no concept of elite races other than Nationals. There were local races people would mark on their calendar that they'd care about and go to year after year, but that was it. It wasn't until the SuperCup that we started to have any sense of elite races throughout the year beyond Nationals."

It is this development as a grassroots movement with a distinct lack of a pro field set apart from the rest that started shifting to a pro scene that makes cyclocross interesting, and what sets it apart from its European ancestry. Statman adds, "The Euros started for different reasons. We adopted it for fun: sort of ironic, hipsterish, and then it got serious. But we've never needed cyclocross for training."

So why don't we need it? Statman explains, "The background and purpose in cyclocross in Europe in the first place is not what happened in the US. I think what happened in Europe is partially Nationalistic, and I think that's the reason we're seeing Belgium have such strong racers today. The Belgians didn't want to leave Belgium in the winter. So cyclocross was a good thing for them and it helped them with races like Paris-Roubaix."

In the US, pro racers had the simple option to leave for warmer climates, all within the 50 states, when the weather turned bad. For Europeans in cyclocross-heavy countries, leaving wasn't as simple, or as attractive, hence the formation of a sport that practically requires inclement weather.

Here, the 'cross scene began as a participant-based sport. Statman believes it's almost become a class structure as years have worn on and elites have become more "pro." Cyclocross continues to grow as the sport to do for recreational riders looking for a bit of excitement, whereas in Europe, that simply isn't the case. "We have a weird class structure in our cyclocross scene. In the US, our pros race 'cross because yeah, it's fun, they fall in love with it, but they don't have the same attitude as the 'lower classes.' For us amateurs, we fall in love with it and so we have a huge participation structure."

At its inception in the US, there weren't long lines at race registration, there were no beer tents. "There was an A race and it could consist of any age category. There was maybe a Masters race, maybe a women's race, and then there was a C race," Stu Thorne explains. "With the advent of the SuperCup in the late 90's, that was a bigger deal, our first national series and the first real elite races."

Cyclocross in the US may have started with the small, local races, but it became a lot more serious with the advent of the SuperCup series in the late 90s. Before the SuperCup, the first national cyclocross series to bring elite level racers together to battle it out before Nationals, the only game in town was Nationals. Veteran pro racer and promoter Jonny "El Gato" Sundt says, "Back then, you raced your region and heard a rumor that someone was going good somewhere else. And then you'd have this big showdown at Nationals."

Andrew Yee agrees, saying, "Going into Nationals, you had a sense of who the favorites were, but because they didn't always have an opportunity to race against each other and test each other, there often were surprises. Unlike today, when people have a dozen opportunities to test themselves against the top talent in the nation and know where they stand."

But then, the SuperCup arrived. Paul Curley explains, "I thought it really took off when we started the SuperCup. It's the first time we got people from different parts of the country to race against each other, other than at Nationals. They were a whole different level. People were doing those races and there wasn't even anything that compared to it on road at the time. It got people to start specializing and prioritizing around cyclocross season."

"SuperCup was very much the early version of the USGP now," Yee explains. "It was the first ever national series of cyclocross races in the US. It finally gave elite racers incentive to travel the nation, it brought top level cyclocross racing to the people. You didn't have to get lucky and have Nationals come to your town. That's when it started to become a big party. People could come and watch high level racing and you can be sure that it was every cyclocross racer's highlight of the season when that came to town."

"I started reading up on 'cross in 2000. Those were the days of the SuperCup series," Mark Vareschi, collegiate promoter in the Eastern Collegiate Cyclocross Conference and the manager for the Rutgers University Cycling Team says. "Tim Johnson was racing, and this was right after he'd gotten that third at Worlds. It was the lead up to where we are in cyclocross now, but it was still very much the early days."

By early 2000, Vareschi says that, "The production value in New England was better than anything I'd done. Courses were taped, and a lot of people were on cyclocross bikes, which I hadn't seen before. At least half of the field was on 'cross bikes. By 2003 though, the New England scene had been around for 20 years already."

THE LEGENDS

Tom Stevens   Photo by Robin MacDonal-Foley

"The elite race wasn't much different," says Stu Thorne. "It was a bunch of guys, six or seven who were core guys, the pros, and then there were guys who did the elite race for fun, just fast local guys. That's not that much different than it is today. I think the fields are a little bigger but it's the same energy and I don't think much has changed in that respect."

Frank McCormack and Jonathan Page
Photo by Robin MacDonal-Foley

Every sport has its legendary riders. In the case of cyclocross, there are names like the McCormack brothers, Laurence Malone, Tom Stevens,

Paul Curley, Ned Overend, Pete Webber, Alison Dunlap, Gina Hall, Brook Watts and countless others. Each region has its local heroes, each scene has its stars, and each state has its champions. Cyclocross has been around for over 40 years in the US, and big names have faded in and out of people's consciousness, in and out of the scene, and in and out of stories told by older racers to newbies and juniors.

"The people winning the races when I started were Paul Curley, Mark and Frank McCormack, Tom Masterson," says Adam Myerson, who's had 20 years of experience to draw from. "Those were my first heroes. Those are the guys I looked up to and learned from."

It's cyclical, and racers learned from racers who learned from racers. For instance, Myerson points out that he was coached by Paul Curley, and both he and Paul Curley helped to coach Jeremy Powers. And when Tim Johnson raced junior Nationals, Frank and Mark McCormack were dueling for the elite National title. A few years later, Johnson would wrestle the title away from the duo. There is much to be said for the women in the sport of cyclocross as well though. Myerson fondly remembers his experiences traveling to Europe at the same time as Anne Grand, now Anne Knapp. "She was really influential to me because she was such a fierce competitor but she always had a good time," he recalls. "She really focused on enjoying what she did, nothing got her down and she bounced back from everything. She had such good perspective that when I was struggling, I really was able to look to her for perspective."

Indeed, it's always been the women from the US, like Alison Dunlap, Gina Hall and, now, Katie Compton who have delivered some of the highest and most consistent results overseas. "Women have been consistently doing well for a long time," Myerson notes. "I think the current generation of spectators don't remember how good the women have been and for how long. We have a handful of women who've been top 10 at Worlds."

One of the best parts about cyclocross is that for some racers, it becomes a lifestyle. Racers like Paul Curley become coaches, racers like Adam Myerson turn into race promoters, and then racers like Geoff Proctor become developers of the future of the sport in our juniors. Proctor fondly remembers his roots in 'cross, saying, "I came to cycling quite late, I was an alpine ski racer. I always rode for training for ski racing, did some road riding, and I was teaching English in Portugal. I flicked on the TV in 1986 and there was the World Championships, from Belgium. It was the most amazing thing I'd ever seen, unbelievably muddy and they were doing probably three-quarters of the lap running."

His voice seems far away as he adds, "I was watching on this big grainy black-and-white TV and I was mesmerized. I thought, 'I've always loved to ride and I'm a good runner, and that looks like a really interesting sport to try.'"

Mark McCormack and Laurence Malone - Photos by Robin MacDonald-Foley

As a native New Englander, Proctor should have had an easy time getting into cyclocross, but he moved to Montana for college. There, he started learning 'cross. "We started teaching ourselves, we pirated videos of Worlds and started teaching ourselves," he says.

"My first Nationals was Plymouth in 1988 and that's when it really started," he remembers. "Then I raced in Switzerland for a couple of years in the early 90s, and raced three World Championships. Kept racing through the 90s but started to turn my eye towards coaching and working with younger riders to help them save all kinds of time and energy." From there, he started coaching kids and founded EuroCrossCamp in 2003.

His shift was a simple decision, as it seemed to be for most of the racers-turned-coaches/promoters/framebuilders/mechanics. "I think I knew that in the big picture, I wanted to help those who were more talented than I am. I felt like I could use my time more wisely by helping out the up-and-comers. These guys, they need someone to be helping them, there really aren't that many people looking out for these guys."

Mark McCormack is another legendary 'cross racer: nearly every pro interviewed for this book mentioned him as either a competitor or as someone he or she looked up to. But for McCormack, getting into cyclocross was simply peer pressure, more than anything else. "Everyone I rode with in 1985 was racing cyclocross," he says, "I figured I should probably give it a try."

Today, he remains nonchalant about his success in the sport. "I guess we were in the right place at the right time and were fortunate that the sport was growing as we were racing," he says of himself and his equally well-known brother, Frank. "We benefited greatly from cyclocross's increased popularity and I am glad that I was able to add some level of entertainment along the way to those that were along for the ride."

One of McCormack's favorite wins was in 1988 at Junior Nationals championship: it took place at his high school. Standout races for Mark McCormack included his first elite Nationals win in 1997, after being trapped in second place many times before. He's also proud of his win in the Saturn Super Cup series in 1998 as the National Champion. He adds, "Gloucester and Boulder were also great wins. Finishing second to [his brother] Frankie in Seattle at Nationals was also a really big race for me."

Of course, not all of the memories of the McCormacks are happy ones. Plenty of older pros have memories of the two demonstrating, with perfect form, the New England style of cyclocross, an aggressive, winner-takes-all style that served them well. Jonny "El Gato" Sundt started racing in 1991, and one of his most clear memories of an early Nationals race was one against the brothers.

Sundt was a racer from across the country, and until Nationals, he didn't have much chance to race against the two. "I started racing mountain bikes, and went down to Seattle," he says. "Being that I love racing way more than I loved training and there was this thing called cyclocross … I started racing 'cross in 1991. So I've been racing for a while. Try racing in toe clips! Clip-in pedals were a game-changer, big time."

While Jeremy Powers is well-known for hopping barriers now, Sundt was hopping them while Powers was still in the junior races. And he was planning on using them to his advantage at Nationals. "The night before the race, I went out, looked at the course and saw the uphill barriers and the triple barrier after it, and I thought, I can hop that. It was twilight and I was j-hopping them. I thought I was going to jump it every lap."

And at the race, he did it. "First lap, I jump it. And the crowd! The New England crowd went ape-shit," he gleefully recalls. "I did it for four laps in a row and they were worried because I was getting a gap. Next lap, I went wide to set it up, and I was a mountain biker so I didn't really know road tactics, but Frank McCormack basically just took a 45 degree angle across my line as he dismounted and made me dismount. The next lap the New England crowd actually boo-ed Frank McCormack. So in that race, he knocked me down, Page ran over me, the pileup from them taking me out is how he won Nationals."

Of course, looking back, Sundt can only laugh and praise the McCormack's fiery style of racing, honed from years of racing on the road and learning that style of tactics. "It's aggressive, I like it," he says.

But how did Sundt end up with a nickname like El Gato? "It was a reporter at some race. I was jumping the barriers and he said I displayed 'catlike skills,' and people got ahold of it and started calling me The Cat," he explains. "And when you hate a nickname, it always sticks. But El Gato was from Todd Wells. Todd evolved the nickname and at that point there was nothing I could do about it."

As an early racer, Sundt was also an early promoter. And for him, looking back to where we've been—he started racing in 1991—it makes him happy to see where we are now. "It's hard to talk about this without feeling like you're patting yourself on the back, but we grew this ourselves. We put on races because we wanted cool events. When we started Starcrossed in 2001, it was because we wanted something cool. So we decided to build it ourselves. Adam [Myerson] was one of the first to bring UCI events to the US, too."

After retiring from the racing scene, Sundt is happy to be done as a racer and working as a rep. Now, he says, "I'll be able to enjoy 'cross more." If anything, he's rekindled the fire. "Being around the USGPs and National scene again made me realize how much I love cyclocross and the people. But of course, there's a mourning period for it. It's a really cool job."

Pete Webber is another one of the oft-cited legends of cyclocross. Still involved in nearly every aspect of the sport, Webber currently helps move 'cross along in Colorado while coaching and still racing. Newcomers to the sport know him as the videographer who starts his interviews with a booming, "Hello, Cyclocross Fans!" before interviewing racers.

"I started 'cross in the early 90's as a way to extend the mountain biking season," he says. "I'd always wanted to try it, but growing up in Maine, there were no 'cross races back then. I moved to Boulder and there was a fully developed race series and plenty of crazy courses. I was hooked straight away."

His first Nationals was in1993, and he came in close second to fellow cyclocross legend Don Myrah. "I was still just a Cat 4 on the road because I was primarily a mountain biker. Everyone was pretty surprised," he laughs. "It poured rain and was just above freezing. People were totally unprepared. The main climb turned into a muck run that took several minutes each lap. I only had one bike and after two laps, the brakes were not functioning at all. There was a downhill dismount and I had to drag a foot on the ground to try and slow down. Needless to say that didn't work too well. I guess that was the start of a long and memorable string of Nationals with ridiculous weather. There have been so many crazy Nationals weather-wise. I mean like extreme tempests, the list is long. Like Golden, Worcester, Kansas City, Portland, Bend, and the most insane: Providence."

That season, his Nationals result was good enough to bring him to Europe as part of the World Championships team. That year, Worlds were held "in a little town in Belgium I'd never heard of: Koksijde." Koksijde was also the site of the 2012 World Championships, which saw a record-setting number of screaming fans lining the course. "We showed up a few days before the race and were pretty amused with the sand," Webber remembers. "We had no idea it was going to be like that. The fans were yelling at me, 'Go home you stupid Yankee!' On the plus side, I pulled into a beer tent right after I got lapped and was immediately given a huge beer. I drank 3/4 of it in one gulp."

Of course, not all legends are racers. The voice of cyclocross, Richard Fries, has been in cycling for over 40 years. While he may not spend much time on the course these days, if you attend any major race in the country, odds are good that you'll hear his booming voice explaining to the crowds what exactly is happening on the course.

He got into cyclocross almost by osmosis: "If you got into cycling in the 70s, you got into all cycling. There were only so many bike riders around and you got to know every one of them. Everybody rode together, so there was a lot more viral transfer of information as to what cycling is, and that meant that you got all of cycling." He pauses and reflects, "I think today people go into cycling and become very channeled. It takes a while before you find other stuff."

And then, the move to New England happened and changed the nature of his involvement in cyclocross. "I was doing really shitty cyclocross in the off season in Florida on a converted road bike, and it was fun. It was just so much fun. Then, I moved to New England and saw my first Nationals in 1988 and it was really cold in Plymouth, Massachusetts. I immediately thought it was the most exciting thing."

Exciting is relative compared to the event that is Nationals today, as Fries explains: "There might have been four categories, I don't know. There was no course tape, just flags and cones here and there, and I watched it and saw great potential for it, I thought it was the coolest thing. I started going to 'cross races and then I started racing 'cross in the 90s. I've only raced about 20 'cross races though, because I quickly transferred into announcing."

So, how did announcing come about? "I raced a lot, for 20 years at a decent level," Fries explains. "Then, I started a magazine. When I was at races as a journalist, I was really disappointed by how bad the announcing was. I was always the guy sitting there narrating under my breath."

Finally, he got on the mic at some road races back in 1995. And as luck would have it, "That year, I was also helping promote the National Championships in Western Massachusetts in Leicester." He laughs, "We did it all at a high school and the stage was planks of wood above the jungle gym on the playground. Bikes were crashing into crowds, wallets were lost, marriages were ruined, ankles were broken. It was the craziest elite men's 'cross race you could have ever fathomed, but it was awesome."

From there, his big break came by way of Lyle Fulkerson, one of the promoters from Nationals. Fulkerson was passionate about sports marketing and promoted the SuperCup series, which took place in big cities like Philadelphia, Chicago, San Francisco, and "it was amazing."

With Fries as the announcer, he says, "I traveled all across America announcing, and local promoters would come to me at races and offer to hire me for their races, so I was suddenly on the national announcing circuit."

For him, taking the announcing gigs was a no brainer. "I was broke. I was making maybe $10,000 a year making my magazine, I had three kids, and trying to raise them on $10,000 a year wasn't easy. Then, I started taking every announcing job I could and while I was traveling, I would work for the magazine. It worked out but it was just hard."

He's been in love with announcing ever since, because it allows him to become the storyteller for any race, whether it's the front of the elite race or the back of the pack in the Cat 4 field. "It's immediate," he says. "The riders respond to announcing. Cyclocross starts as a road race and ends as a boxing match, It ends up with these one-on-one battles, or these small little groups, and the stories become that much better. It's so intense."

Building cyclocross in the US from scratch, in a way that's distinctly American, is part of its charm. "It was something that was built by people," Sundt says, dreamily. "It's a 'for life' thing."

CYCLOCROSS IN EUROPE

Cyclocross differs wildly between here and in Europe in more ways that simplify its origin story. Because of the way racing works in Europe, as more of a passive spectator sport for all but the highest elite level racers as opposed to the participant-heavy style of the sport in the US, the courses there are designed with pro athletes in mind, so tend to be more technical in nature.

Richard Fries has been the English voice announcing Cyclocross Worlds, and while it's one of the highest honors an announcer from the US could achieve, for him, the racing in Europe is lacking the same spark that racing in the US has. "I don't want to sound flip but announcing it was incredibly disappointing. You're in a closet, talking to a TV, because that's how it's covered." However, Fries did try to change the nature of announcing and found that it worked: "I loved going out before the race with the microphone and I've gotten the European announcers to go out of their box, and just walk around and talk to people. I enjoy that and I love being there. I love being on a run-up with a wireless microphone."

At the end of the day though, it's the participant-based nature of 'cross in the US that Fries missed: "I love calling a Women's 3/4 race as much as I like announcing the pro race."

European racing is a different ballgame also in terms of how the racers respond to the crowd, and the salaries that they bring in because of the crowd. "When you have tens of thousands of non-participant spectators paying good money to watch a race in the middle of winter, that just ups the game and importance," says Andrew Yee, adding that it "focuses all the attention on the riders and the winners, and makes it very attractive to corporations and it becomes a very serious sport."

It's not just the announcing and spectating that's different though. Brook Watts explains that the racing is slightly different as well. "The racing is harder over there, there's a different flow from the race. In America, the holeshot is everything, and the race is raced off the front," he says. "Euro races tend to be a little more tactical. We're amazed in America when there's a group of four or five riders who stay together and the race develops in the last half of the race."

For elite racers, racing overseas is a whole different ball game, to confuse sports metaphors. For some, it's better, and for some, it's harder. For all of them, it's a whole different world.

> "It's faster, the courses are a lot harder, more technical, and the culture is different too. Cycling, to the people in Belgium, that's their thing. That's what they do for entertainment; they go watch the races. I think the biggest thing is the courses, how technical they are. In Namur, I stood on top of this drop for ten minutes before I was brave enough to go down it, whereas here, you wouldn't see anything like that."
> —Kaitie Antonneau

> "It's just the elites and juniors. You don't have the other categories. It's just all for us, which is nice. There's still a huge fan contingency even though it's just elites, so there are a lot of people but more in the purely spectator sense. It's a little more aggressive and the course designers aren't afraid of throwing in a few gnarly elements, they can really get away with throwing the harder elements in there. It's nice because you get those more challenging features."
> —Nicole Duke

> "I've done Worlds since when I was in the 17-18 field, so I've done Worlds five times now, and I spent two and a half months out of the season in Europe as a junior, living and racing. It's hard for the Americans over there because we have to deal with the culture shock, and that's always the biggest hurdle. Everyone describes that instead of the racing itself. Everyone says it's different, it's loud, there are tons of people, different courses and a bigger field but a lot of that comes from the culture shock of just not being European. If you break it down to the actual racing, it's just really fast, solid

guys. They have a bigger pool to choose from because more people do it as an actual lifestyle. That's how they get the huge number of good guys. It's like football. If you try out 10,000 guys, you're going to find 100 really good guys, but if you try out 100 guys, you'll probably only find one or two good guys. Same thing applies with European racing. It's a lifestyle over there, more well known. Once you get over the culture shock, it's still just pedaling your bike in mud, sand, snow, same thing as here but you don't speak the language."
                                                                    –Luke Keough

It's like Nascar versus Formula One. They're both racing but it feels so different. In the US it's so participation based. They don't want to talk about the pros and who's going to beat who. They talk about their own race, their own training, their own equipment. Whereas over in Europe, it feels very professional but you don't get that same connection. You can't talk to the guy next to you about his ride that week because he's probably fat and smoking a cigar."
                                                                    –Colt McElwaine

"In my opinion, they're really two separate leagues. Here we have super dry, really fast with a lot of turns. In Europe, historically it's always wet, there's a lot of mud and it's a different style of racing. Really, they are two separate things. They're the same in that they're both cyclocross races and we're doing the same thing by name, but one is mud 'cross and the other is fast 'cross. The guys that come from Europe don't do as well here because it's different events and we don't do well there because it's different events. And when you start to cross-pollinate them, over the years and see more US in Europe and more Europe in the US, you'll get one type of racing that's similar. I think that the courses have more long power sections; they're a little more difficult in Europe in terms of obstacles. We're harder in that we have lots of short power sections, the efforts are in short bursts. In Europe you get two or three minute straights, all out. Plus, obviously, there's also the cultural shock of just being in Europe, so there's a ton of stuff that comes into play when you're racing in Europe."   –Jeremy Powers

"It was so exciting and overwhelming over there so I couldn't compare it to anything over here."   –Laura Van Gilder

"I haven't raced much cyclocross internationally, but I have spent a ton of time racing the mountain bike there. I would say there are two main differences. The depth of the field in Europe is huge. Because there are so many great riders, the time gaps between riders are small and that makes for much more aggressive racing. I don't know if it's racing or just the culture over there. People don't give much personal space anywhere so it makes sense that you are constantly fighting for position there. The courses also seem to be much more challenging there. In the US, courses have to be rideable for everyone from the pros to the weekend warriors. Promoters make a lot of their money on entry fees so the course has to be pretty mellow. In Europe, only the best riders are even able to compete and there are rarely citizens races so the courses are much more challenging."   –Todd Wells

"The competition in the US is good but it drops off faster than it does in Europe. The numbers at the level are deeper. There, you're fighting tooth and nail for a podium position or for 40th place. You're throwing elbows the whole time and if you're sprinting for 42nd place, someone will be sprinting with you. I think in Europe it's just more aggressive. In the US, you can say, 'on your left' and people will move over for you. In Europe, you say that, they'd probably move into you."   –Amy Dombroski

"I think they're pretty similar, even at the World Cup level. There are more people at the same ability in Europe. In the US, we have the top 10 or 12 women who aren't that far apart, and on any given day, five people could win. Then there's a bit of a jump to the next ability level. In Europe, you take that 10 to 12 and there's 30 of them."   —Mo Bruno Roy

"I've done everything from Belgian B races up to the World Cups. I've done the races with the biggest crowds and it's scary. At home, I can block the crowd out when it's loud and focus on what I'm doing. I don't feel as on stage, though it's increased in recent years. Now, when I race outside of the New England region, the response that I get from spectators is really surprising and I'm still not used to it. They're psyched to see you and psyched to cheer for you, even if you're having a bad day. I have started to feel more like a performer and I'm more conscious of the crowd. But in Europe, the fans didn't race that morning. When you're in a World Cup and everyone is paying $10 to be there and you're in front of 10,000 people, you really feel like a professional athlete. You feel different when kids are coming up and asking for your trading card and it can make you nervous. When you make mistakes, you're making them in front of people, you're making them on TV. It can take you off your game."   —Adam Myerson

"Bicycles are part of their culture. People relate to the bike, so 'cross guys over there are like rock stars. The whole family goes to races and treat it like they're going to see the ball game. In the US, there are very few people there just to watch, and if they are, they probably know somebody. It's a social event. There are plenty of people who go and don't watch the race, they're just there to socialize and drink."   —Stu Thorne

"It's a participatory versus spectator model, and what that means in the US is that the courses tend to not be as daunting as the Euro courses are, which presents a challenge for race directors in the US, since we want to have courses that prepare riders for Europe but still provide opportunities for a junior or Cat 4 rider. The races are much more tactical, a little more wait-and-see. There's a more even distribution of talent among the top eight or so riders, so they can be that group who sits until someone makes a move. But more than anything, it's the type of spectator we get, and that sets the tone for what makes our races different."   —Brook Watts

3: THE STATE OF CYCLOCROSS TODAY

"I used to race road bikes and mountain bikes and track bikes but now I just race cross." –Molly Cameron

In the past few years, racing cyclocross as a primary sport rather than as off-season training has become more and more popular. Racers like Jonathan Page pioneered the trend, electing to make the move from the US, where cyclocross racers remained underpaid and hard-pressed to find big races, to Belgium, where big races happen within a 100 mile radius weekly, with bigger prize lists and start money for bigger name racers. Page was one of those racers, having taken a bronze medal at Elite Men's Worlds: the only US male to do so.

However, racing 'cross in the US isn't a new phenomenon, though its popularity certainly is. Nationals in the US date back to the mid-1970s, though it wasn't until the past fifteen years that the National Championship came to hold the same meaning that it does now.

'Cross in the US has come and gone. It started as a fringe sport, became popular, hit another downward slump, and in the past few years, has skyrocketed to popularity in the US again. The level of the pro field has come up, and now there are pros who can take cyclocross seriously as their primary sport, and can do so almost entirely domestically. For the pros who were doing cyclocross as a secondary sport, they're feeling the levels rise with the popularity of cyclocross, and are forced to rise to the occasion or accept that they need to drop back to lower level fields in smaller races.

Geoff Kabush is one of those athletes: "Cyclocross was on a high with the Supercup in 1997, then I think it hit a lull. But now it's come back really strong. It's tough for me because guys are taking it more seriously, but it's really great to see that guys can focus on it now and make that a job. When I started, there wasn't anyone who was a full time 'crosser, so much as roadies and MTBers that just had a passion for it. It's cool to see specialists able to make a living doing it, but at the same time it makes my job a littler harder to do. I definitely have to take it more seriously now."

Coaches like Geoff Proctor, who try to push juniors towards careers in 'cross, have taken notice of the shift and are thankful. "It seemed like for a while that road and mountain bike took precedent, but guys are seeing that to do well in 'cross in January they can't keep killing themselves all year on road," he says. "And you have to get them to think about that so they can structure things so they can keep doing well in January. It's even hard now for the juniors I work with to be fresh by late January. It takes conscious thinking and planning."

In the past few years, with the advent of pro cyclocross coming into its own as a sport where elite racers can make a living, and with the rising popularity of more "extreme" sports like mud runs, CrossFit and now, cyclocross, as Amy Dombroski says, "Every year, it grows exponentially."

Promoters like Dorothy Wong agree, and are seeing rising participant numbers. "The sport is not peaked by any means, I think it's still growing. We've had a steady growth of 25% for the past two or three years, so I think it'll definitely continue to grow."

Perhaps this growth is attributable, as CXHairs Bill Schieken believes, to the fact that, "Cyclocross is the kid who moves between tribes. Everyone can get into it."

One thing all of the pros agree about in terms of cyclocross is that it has the highest level of accessibility compared to other forms of cycling, which can be daunting to some, and just plain uncool to others. Schieken adds, "When you're a Cat 5 on the road, there's sort of a stigma attached to that. In cyclocross, people that are new seem perfectly comfortable there."

And it's this accessibility that makes cyclocross fun for everyone, from the seasoned racer to the five-year-old in Kiddie Cross to the too-cool-for-school teenager on a single-speed in jeans. "It's becoming a primary sport for people. It seems like cyclocross, now, for many people is the entry point," Schieken says. "You see it with kids, and you see it with hipsters starting with cyclocross. I just started a team and I have 20 hipsters on it. This is where they start. They go in and want to wear their cutoff jeans and then two years later, they're shaving their legs and racing a crit and doing intervals. And it's like, 'Wait a second! Two years ago you were smoking a cigarette and hanging out on a track bike.'"

For those new to the sport, it hasn't always been as big in the US as it is now. Ryan Trebon remembers, "Five years ago, Barry and I were traveling by ourselves with our bikes and wheels to races, and now we're showing up and there's team trucks and the presentation looks good, there are mechanics, we don't have to worry about stuff. It's awesome. It's going good. I think sometimes the younger riders don't quite grasp what it used to be like and they want too much."

Now that the sport is growing, the sanctioning body, USA Cycling, has been working to grow the sport. Andrew Yee, the founder of *Cyclocross Magazine,* says that, "Lately, USA Cycling has impressed me with how they've brought cyclocross to the people through increased media attention, through their online streaming video coverage of the National Championships, by bringing UCI promoters to a summit to discuss cyclocross issues, and by giving further recognition to aspects of the sport like single-speed racing."

However, with all of the growth that cyclocross has seen, Yee thinks that there is more to be done. "The long healthy growth of cyclocross and the fact that the majority of those races are USA Cycling sanctioned, I feel like a greater portion of those proceeds should go back to developing grassroots cyclocross racing and make it more accessible and affordable to more people, not just go towards supporting elite racers in their efforts to go to World Championships, or worse, have these funds redirected to road, mountain or track disciplines."

As a racer and promoter for 20 years, Adam Myerson has a lot to say on the subject of how far the sport has come. For one, he believes that, "The level of production of the events themselves has increased dramatically. Our game has gotten better."

He continues, "We're concerned about how things look and the sturdiness of our infrastructure. When we started, surveyors flags were enough to mark the course. Now, you're not just marking the course, you're trying to separate racers and spectators, it's actual crowd control."

It isn't just about creating a better course for racers now though. Instead, Myerson says, "We're also concerned about how things look visually, in photos and in video, for sponsor representation. 15 years ago, there were 150 people showing up at the courses, we got up at 6 am and set up the course that morning. Now we start setting courses up three days before the race and they're semi-permanent installations. As a race organizer, that's a big change."

It's not just an organic growth of cyclocross domestically. Without the various race series around the country stepping up their game in recent years, the cyclocross world wouldn't be nearly as developed. Statman points out, "The biggest difference in the last five years is directly attributable to what's going on in the New England, Mid-Atlantic and USGP series, in that those races have really stepped up their game. And now, Nationals is a big deal. When I went to Bend, I had never heard so many people screaming and cheering." Next, we're taking a look at a few of the race series that have sprouted up in the US, and how they've affected the sport."

It's not just Nationals that are becoming more of a big scene. Local series are stepping up their game, and the push to create separate-but-equal pro and amateur series is most obvious in the New England region with the creation of the Verge New England Cyclo-Cross Series and the Shimano New England Pro Cyclocross Series, which both grew out of the Verge Series of years past. Because of the growing popularity of cyclocross and the rising numbers of racers, both in the elite and amateur fields, race directors are finding it challenging to accommodate all of the racers' needs: hard, challenging courses and big prize purses to draw top-level elites and courses that won't terrify (or grievously injure) a true novice who's out for a day of fun with the family.

Even the juniors who are relatively new to the sport have noticed a significant growth. Luke Keough, who's been racing bikes for most of his life, but only racing cyclocross for five years now, says that, "New England has blown up, the Northwest has a new scene and I've seen it develop over the years." He explains, adding, "I was at Providence for two Nationals years ago and it was nothing compared to the UCI race [part of the Shimano New England Pro Cyclocross Series] that was there this year. We're also finally getting sponsors—not just in the industry but from outside support—and it's being recognized as something to follow."

Todd Wells, Olympic mountain bike racer and National Champion, has been watching cyclocross grow for over 15 years, and says, "I think it was fairly big with the Super Cup back in the late 90s but the USGP has upped the level again."

Even though he's a mountain biker, Wells is quick to admit that cyclocross has taken on the feeling that mountain biking had in its heyday. "I think that 'cross has the feel right now that MTB had back in early 90s, it's the 'in' thing in the cycling community." Perhaps part of the reason for this is that sites like *CyclingDirt* and *Cyclocross Magazine* have upped the ante in providing fast coverage, sometimes even live feeds of events. Wells says, "I bet 90% of US Pro road and MTB cyclists watched the National Championships live this year online. It has made it more accessible to everyone."

It's also become more accessible as a lifestyle for a pro racer. "From a racing standpoint, when I started in the late 80s, there were only 30 of us showing up for the races and we all raced together: elites, masters, women and juniors," Myerson recalls. "The juniors, masters and women finished at 40 minutes and the elites went an extra 15 minutes. To go from that to consistently getting 500-800 racers at a Verge race, obviously the popularity has changed." This increase in popularity has not only helped promoters, it's helped racers: "The exposure has changed, the amount of coverage we get has changed, and at an elite level, the salaries have changed. 'Cross is finally viable from an earning potential standpoint."

Andrew Yee agrees, adding, "Here in the States, a handful of guys can make it their entire focus and make a living at it, there's no better sign than that that the sport has grown from its early days."

However, it's still not quite as viable if a racer is trying to stay domestic. To compete against the best in the world, racers are essentially forced to spend a portion of the season in Europe. Paul Curley used to race in Europe when he first started in the 80s, and even now, he thinks for a racer to make it, spending time in Europe is necessary. "I think if they want to do international level racing, if they want to race against the fastest people in the world, they're going to have to go to Europe because those people aren't all going to come here, with the exception of Worlds." He adds, "I think someone can be a very good racer just racing in the US but they won't be a great racer internationally."

THE COURSES TODAY

In the US, when you talk to elite racers about the courses, ultimately they all tend to agree on one major point: the courses are "dumbed down" compared to those in Europe. The key difference is simple: in Europe, only the elite racers are on course, so the obstacles and barriers can be made harder and more dangerous. In the US, because it's a participant sport, the 75-year-old master and 10-year-old junior are riding the same course as the top elite riders, and so the dangerous elements tend to be removed. Because of that, often, racers claim that the courses can be too easy.

© Dejan Smaic

"In the US, you have a roadie-style course or a 'dirt crit,' which isn't a negative comment, it's a descriptive comment," Mo Bruno Roy says. "People get insulted but it's a legitimate description of course style in the US. Then you have a hilly race, or technical race, and there are descriptors for races. In Europe, all of the races are geared toward being challenging for elite riders."

"We race in parks. They're manicured parks. In Europe, it could be in someone's field that just got plowed, with a really gnarly downhill. It's not that it's better, it's just different," Stu Thorne elaborates. "In the US, you have everyone racing on the same course, from Tim Johnson to a first-time racer. If you go over there, typically there's maybe three or four races in a day instead of 12 like we have here. So our courses get a bit dumbed down here, I think."

When designing a course, making it as spectator-friendly as possible is key. Because the US promoters want to encourage people to stay and watch the race, hard sections of the course need to be on display and easy to walk to. This adds a new layer of toughness to a race, since every mistake a rider makes is on full display. "It's so easy to pull out of a road race," Richard Fries explains. "You're 40 miles out, you're on a shitty climb, there's no one else there. Same with mountain biking. It's so easy to cave in."

He pauses. "But in 'cross, you have some shithead with a cowbell on course screaming at you and you can't quit. Your weakness will have witnesses and I think it drives people on to do things. I love getting every drop of stuff out of a rider. Even if they're racing for 28th place."

THE MEDIA TODAY

It's nearly impossible to find old accounts of National Championships, local races, or even how our racers did in World Championships. However, with the rise of online journalism and the growing popularity of the sport, as well as the over-the-top nature of some of the riders involved, in recent years there has been a growth in the cyclocross media industry. Among the publications following cyclocross, there's *Cyclocross Magazine* (cxmagazine.com), a print and online magazine devoted to year-round cyclocross coverage including race reporting of every major UCI race during the season; *CyclingDirt* (cyclingdirt.org), which features basic race coverage but more importantly, features interviews and highlight reels of races all over the country, and countless smaller sites like *In The Crosshairs* (cxhairs.com), which are more locally-oriented sites dedicated to providing information, interviews and reports from a specific region.

Andrew Yee founded *Cyclocross Magazine* in the fall of 2007, and when asked why, at first he says that, "Temporary insanity is the first thing that comes to mind."

He sobers up, and explains, "I started this publication because I wanted to help. I wanted to see the sport grow, and it was something I was just passionate about. I was just craving any media attention on the sport and was never satisfied with the amount that there was. You come to a point where you realize that no one is going to do it, so you're going to have to do it yourself."

Apart from CyclocrossWorld, which by then was focusing on product rather than news, there were very little options available. Yee says, "I was always absolutely coveting every mention of cyclocross. If they had a single piece about a race or a rider, you can guarantee that I kept it and read it ten times over. Even though the sport has grown in participation and bike options, five years ago in 2007, I still didn't see much attention on the sport."

And then, the 'temporary insanity' struck, hard. "Sometimes, to get what you want, you just have to do it yourself, so we created a website and a print magazine," he says. "My goal was to expose the sport to more people, show the sport to more fans, and provide an in-depth, objective way to get people to emotionally get more into the sport."

The magazine started coming out quarterly, and to Yee, the best part is that, "People look to us as an authority and respect our content, online and in print, appreciate the fact that we do in-depth content, objective reviews and really interviews, because that's really rare in this day and age."

Additionally, the website has provided daily content and race coverage of every major UCI race worldwide during the season, and Yee couldn't be more pleased with the reaction of readers. "Across the board, I have just been completely amazed with how the cyclocross community has embraced us and how we've made a difference in the cyclocross community," he says. "That, to me, every day when I work on this labor of love, is incredible motivation to make it even better and continue on this path. It's absolutely confirmation that this decision was the right one."

From the local side of things, Bill Schieken runs *In The Crosshairs* to promote cycling in the DC area. The site has evolved since its inception, though the premise has remained the same. "I got into 'cross in 2007," Scheiken explains, "And at the time I was working on a publication about government contracting, which is not the most exciting topic in the world. We were interviewing, writing these stories, so I had these skills."

The natural progression happened, and while racing cyclocross, Schieken says, "I thought it would be cool to do that type of interviews, that type of writing, for something that was actually interesting."

"My take on it was that I wanted to capture the experience, but I didn't want it to be about me," he continues. "I had done some work for *Cyclocross Magazine* with Nationals interviews so I started doing those interviews at local races. Sending out questions, interviewing people, and then putting up these interviews and stories. If you were on the podium, I was sending you an email, and whoever responded, I would put it out there. And that seemed to be popular."

While the site started as a primarily interview-focused site, that shifted as Schieken began to experiment. "I did the helmet-cam stuff for a year. I like finding new fun things and moving on to something different. So I got into putting out the videos of each race, some video interviews and stuff. And that's what I've been doing for the last year." Like many other cyclocross-devoted websites, it'll never be a major moneymaker, but it's a passion project that keeps Schieken happily involved in the sport.

And rather than going national, Schieken knows that for him, he'd rather keep it local. "I thought it would be cool to put a spotlight on the grassroots, the local heroes, as opposed to the national scene," he says.

Cyclocross media is still in early stages of development in the US, and like the sport itself, the coverage relies on grassroots support from fans, supporters, elite and amateur racers alike.

4: RACES & SERIES IN THE U.S.—FROM CROSS VEGAS TO THE VERGE SERIES

"Give the racers what they want, not just what you want. I see a lot of promoters' events go stale. They don't ever change them up or offer anything new or different. Racers are just like everyone else, they like it when the pillow gets fluffed now and then." —Murphy Mack, race promoter

Road racing has the Giro D'Italia, the Tour de France, Paris Roubaix, and too many others to count. And in the States, there's the Tour de Grove, the Amgen Tour of California, and the USA Crits series. On a worldwide scale, cyclocross has no races quite as well known as the Tour, though Cyclocross World Championships have seen spectator crowds of over 60,000 screaming fans. Still, we can't talk about the racers who make cyclocross in the US great without first talking about some of the first and most prominent race series in the country. After all, if you had never heard of the Tour de France, it wouldn't mean too much to know Lance had won it, now would it?

If you're new to cycling, the fact that races are UCI-designated or not might not mean anything. But if you're serious about racing your bike and want to "go pro" at some point, you are hunting UCI points with a burning passion. Luckily, in the US, UCI-ranked cyclocross races are getting easier and easier to find, though typically the races are primarily found on either the East or West Coast, while the middle of the country is working hard to catch up. However, not everyone is happy with the growing number of UCI races in the US, and some have suggested that we have too many.

However, most believe that having these big races to pull in big pros (including top European racers) will only serve to elevate cycling in the US. For example, USA Cycling representative Marc Gullickson is pro-UCI races. He says, "One of the main things is that we're trying to encourage and not stifle the promoters interested in putting on UCI races."

In fact, he argues that, "While there are some people who think we have too many UCI races, I think that the fact that we have such a big country and such big regions with cyclocross means that we don't have that many when you look at our land mass. I think the UCI races are how we tie cyclocross in all these regions together. Thankfully, a lot of our best riders travel around to those races."

And thankfully, the promoters who put on the races tend to be devoted, body and soul, to making cyclocross a major part of cycling in the US. "The people that are involved in this sport and the names that you read about every weekend, and the amount of their personal lives and efforts thrown into it is just unbelievable," Jonny Sundt says.

Promoters have had to decide which direction that they want their race to take. For every big race, a local race has crept into the calendar as well, and that distinction, between grassroots races and big elite races, has started to widen. "I think what you're seeing is big races getting bigger and small races getting smaller," Adam Myerson says. "Racers are choosing to go one way or another, to do a low budget production and try not to lose any money, or bring in big sponsors. We need both of those things: we need big weekends, we need low-key weekends."

Cyclocross promoters cross-pollinate ideas amongst themselves, and constantly work to better their races, often by taking cues from other promoters. Promoter Richard Fries emphasizes this point, saying, "As a promoter, I want to say my race is going to be the best race in America, and I know that my friend Joan Hanscom is saying the exact same thing about her USGP and Brook Watts is saying that about his races. And we should all be trying, and trying to learn from each other."

While in some sectors of racing, like road, USA Cycling has the first and last word in race promotion, in cyclocross, the governing organization has, thus far, been perfectly content to take a backseat role and watch the growth happen organically. "I think we've let the free market just work its magic and the promoters are always doing more," Gullickson says. "It's great to see cyclocross promoters proceed with the UCI designation and prize money and value. And I think that the cycling media really gets behind the 'cross season and they do get a lot of press, and those top racers are following the UCI calendar in the US."

So what US-based series play host to these UCI races?

SHIMANO NEW ENGLAND PRO CYCLOCROSS SERIES AND VERGE SERIES

Most series in the US started simply: grassroots races run by racers looking to get in extra practice in the off-season, or just racers who love cyclocross. For a racer like Adam Myerson, his reasons for wanting to help run a series were simple. When he took over running the Verge series in the late 90s, turning it into a full UCI series by early 2000, his motivation was simple: "I've always put all of this effort into building a playground I wanted to play in, so it felt really good at this point in my career to have this really mature series that's meeting all of the goals that I'd set out for it. It's like I built my own skate park and finally got to skate it."

Myerson started promoting races at the University of Massachusetts in Amherst, where he says, "I was super into 'cross, and people get evangelical about 'cross and want to get everyone into it." He was part of their cycling team, and says that they had a mountain bike race that "had potential to be a really great cyclocross race," despite being a less than stellar mountain bike race.

He says, "Everyone chipped in to the club in one way or another, so I offered to turn the mountain bike race into a cyclocross race with a guy named Mike Horner, and that's how UMass cyclocross was born."

Why cyclocross? "There's a difference between what's fun to do and what's fun to watch," he says. "And I think what makes 'cross successful is that it does both of those things well. With 'cross you get a fun, fast, challenging course, and you can spectate the whole thing. I think that's why it has the perfect recipe."

Originally, the race was run at UMass and acted as the Eastern Collegiate Cyclocross Championships for a few years. "Before Gloucester was big, the biggest races in New England were UMass and Putney," Myerson explains. "It was the big weekend, we were the first to break 500 racers and that was the mid-90s. Eventually, we changed the weekend, and then we combined with Farmington, another UCI race." Now, that race is Cycle-Smart International.

Of course, if you ask Myerson how he managed to take hold of the series, he's the first to say, "I'll tell you right now it's the dumbest thing I ever did and if I could go back right now, I would never have done it."

"Despite all the things that people want to give me credit for about how much I've affected the sport," he continues, "I think it has 100% come at my expense and I'm not sure what I came out with at the end. It was a compulsion from the beginning, the way a writer has to write all day or an artist has to fill a sketchbook. From day one, I don't know why or how, but I guess it was just my nature. If I see something that could be better, I can't help but try to make it better."

Gloucester is considered New England Worlds on the East Coast.

© Pedal Power Photography

For a long time, every race in New England was part of the New England points series, which eventually turned into the Verge Series. However, races eventually began to split off from the series. "When we started getting UCI races, Putney decided to stay small and UMass decided to get bigger." It eventually changed to Cycle-Smart International, since Myerson's coaching company, Cycle-Smart, was the company fronting the money for the race.

New England has taken a lot of heat for having such a high density of UCI races in the region [see page 216]. Myerson has fought to keep the UCI races that have been running in New England continuing, despite push-back from other promoters and even from the UCI. He doesn't see the number of UCI races in the area as a problem, however. "People talk about how the US has more UCI races than Belgium, but all the races in Belgium are in one tiny part of Belgium. When Massachusetts has 50 races, we can talk about comparing it to Belgium," he argues. "If you look at land and population density, 14 races in Massachusetts is absolutely appropriate. And you can see the quality of riders develop because we run races that serve riders at all levels."

Last year, Myerson began to realize that, "It's difficult to make everyone happy with every event." For him, when the UCI enforced its rule of eight UCI-designated races per series, it was an opportunity to split the series from the Verge Series into the Verge Series and Shimano Series, and do something no other promoter had done: shift the focus of each series to a different demographic. So, "The Shimano Series will still serve everyone, but its priority will be professionals. Verge will still have professional racing, but the priority will be the grassroots categories."

Cycle-Smart International is now in its 23rd year, and the times have changed the course, not only by shifting its location, but in terms of who's racing and who's watching. "The first year I did it, there weren't any spectators," Myerson recalls. "I don't even think family members came out, it was 30 dudes in a field. Within five years, we had 500 racers and probably an equal amount of spectators. We're only just now starting to get spectators that didn't also race, but I think it's growing steadily over the years."

He proudly adds, "Now I think we get 1000 or 2000 spectators, and that's a pretty big crowd. It's enough to make some noise and make the event look big."

US GRAND PRIX OF CYCLOCROSS

© Dejan Smaic

When the SuperCup ceased to exist as a national series, the void was filled by the US Grand Prix of Cyclocross [USGP]. "I think the USGP series does an amazing job right now as far as visibility," said elite racer Geoff Kabush.

When nearly all of the elite racers in the country are willing to travel to your race series, you know you're doing something right. The USGP series is the only series in the US that travels to different, far-flung locations over the course of the season. In the 2011 season, races were in Wisconsin, Oregon, Colorado, and Kentucky, and the best of the best of the elite field flocked to each city for weekends full of serious racing.

"Back in 2006, we had just launched our cycling production company," co-promoter Joan Hanscom explains. "We put out a press release and Bruce Fina, the founder of USGP, contacted us and asked if we wanted to work with him on the USGP. I had never produced a cyclocross race, but had done big road races. We did that season and my first race was Gloucester and I was totally blown away. I thought, 'Oh my God, this is the coolest thing I've ever seen,' and 'Wow, we can do a lot with this.'"

As a promoter, Hanscom was instantly drawn to the sport. "The thing that I saw right away is how spectator-friendly it is," she says, and admits that she loves, "how easy it is. It's a lot of hard work, but compared to shutting down 12 miles of street in San Francisco, having a contained venue is pretty nice. You don't have to inconvenience citizens, and that's nice."

"As a person with a background of doing pretty big events, I could see where cyclocross was a spectator-friendly, fun to watch, fun to race event. Looking at it, I thought, 'This is magic in a bottle.'"

The USGP isn't just about the elite racers, and Hanscom says, "We provide a really quality race experience for everyone who comes out to race. So we have the same announcers announcing for the 10-12 Juniors as are announcing for the pros, so everyone feels like they get that really pro experience all day long. And we want to execute well. We try to execute to the letter of the UCI law and make quality courses."

That said, Hanscom realizes that the USGP is more focused on the pro field than the amateurs at the race. "Part of the founding principle of the USGP was to create head-to-head competition weekend in and weekend out at the top pro level. That was the mission when we started," Hanscom says, and the pros that race in the series are happy to say that their mission is accomplished.

The USGP has filled an important role in cyclocross in the US: it allows the big racers to scope out competition before Nationals. "We had it great when we had a couple of series going, and we're all thankful that the USGP is still providing us with a national series that all the top racers can converge on," Andrew Yee says.

Building the sport is one of their priorities, and holding races big enough to bring in attention from mainstream media is important to Hanscom. "I remember our first year I worked on the USGP, we had an article in the New York Times. But those are few and far between," she says. The problem, she adds, is simply that cyclocross is still a very niche sport in the US, as opposed to the celebrity-culture it has in Europe. Even with livestreaming of races, it's still hard to get people outside of the small group of cyclocrossers to watch. "If you give people the opportunity to see it, that's the hard part. We have livestreaming of our races and good viewership, but how do you take that out of your specific niche?" she asks.

To do it, she believes that changing how people in the US look at our top racers is key: "You have to create a certain celebrity-athlete culture to get people to want to watch it." To that end, she thinks people like Jeremy Powers with his *Behind THE Barriers* reality show, and websites like *CyclingDirt,* are helping to make that possible.

But for Hanscom and other US promoters, with the bad, there is a major upside: "Part of the great thing about US cycling is that it's a participation sport. They lack that in Belgium. People in Belgium aren't racing their bikes earlier in the day."

For a promoter, that means money isn't coming in from participants like it is in the case of the USGP, it's coming from spectators. "They get 68,000 people out to watch the World Championships, but how is the sport growing when you're not feeding it on a participation base too? I would never want to see 'cross in the US lose that participatory base, but I would like to see spectators grow."

National Champion Jeremy Powers says, "I think the USGP is clearly the best series so far and it's given us a great opportunity to do this thing for real for a while, and given us a great chance to showcase ourselves and cyclocross. And all of these grassroots series springing up in all these areas of the countries are creating such great scenes, there's so much going on."

SO CAL CYCLOCROSS

"It's kind of a different scene down there," Portland-based elite racer Molly Cameron says. "In Portland and Seattle, that's it: those are the hubs. They're all within two or three hours from each other and there's nothing else in Washington, that's where the 'cross racing is. In SoCal, LA is so ridiculously big, it's a funny scene down there."

Promoter Dorothy Wong has been heavily involved in the evolution of the SoCal racing scene since she started racing obsessively in 1997. "All I wanted to do was race," she explains. "Today, a lot of people just add it to what they're doing, but I fell into it when it wasn't quite the explosion that it's become. I've been racing 'cross nonstop since then."

Her career didn't begin in Southern California, simply because there wasn't a scene there at the time. Forced to travel to race, Wong picked up bits and pieces of what makes 'cross work in various regions and brought them home with her. She also learned a lot about the difference between UCI events and non-UCI events, an issue that plagues California race promoters now. "I started traveling around, doing the Redline Cups, a West Coast series. I'd love to see something like that come back," she explains. "I traveled around and was going to the National Championships—since 1999, I had raced every National Championship that there was—and I got to see the different cultures."

From that, Wong and several other cyclocross-minded people came up with the concept of starting to grow the sport in a more serious way in their region. "So to make it grow in Southern California, we started thinking that we should put on quality cyclocross racing in Southern

California and it started spreading. We were all putting on races and unified so we'd have a series in Southern California," she explains. "About nine years ago, we put on a race called Turkey Trot. It was Thanksgiving-themed and that sparked the growth of the series. Since then it's evolved into adding a couple of UCI weekends to the mix."

To say Wong was a natural promoter is an understatement. In the business world, promoting events is essentially her day job. "Coming from entertainment television and putting on live events—that was my job—it was just like putting on a television show in a lot of ways. It was a natural thing to do."

Starting a series in a mostly warm and dry climate hasn't been easy, and neither has gaining acceptance as a "real" cyclocross region. But promoters have learned to work with what they have, and make the most of the conditions. "Our reality is that honestly, our Southern California Series wants the mud, they want the conditions that are really some of the best dynamic parts of cyclocross. For us though, we're hard packed, dry, dusty racing. That's just our reality."

Since the start of the series, the promoters are thrilled to have over 20 races in the area, including a few scattered UCI events, and 400 to 500 racers at each race. "The pressure is to produce bigger events now," Wong says.

Unlike the scene in New England, SoCal is tasked with trying to create a more festive atmosphere at events to draw amateur racers, and there's less of a focus on the elite level.

"The reality still is that you want to get the community to come, so to me, the challenge of the promoter is to put on more than a 'cross race, period. Not just market it as a cyclocross race," she says. For SoCal, the challenge isn't drawing the elite riders, because they'll come regardless. For her, it's about bringing the community into the racing scene.

To do this, as with most things in Hollywood, it's *location, location, location*. "The challenge for a cyclocross promoter is getting the 'cross race into a populated section of the community," Wong argues. "It's easier to put on the event on private property. But it's the way you market it to the community. We know what cyclocross is but does anyone else? And do they really care?"

Wong believes that the sport has grown in leaps and bounds within the cycling community, but it's the non-cyclists that she now wants to target to grow her races. "I think as promoters grow, they have the dynamic to define the sport. It will evolve into different things," she says, and for her, she wants it to evolve into a fun-for-the-whole-family style of event.

"It's great because everyone can race: mom, dad, the kids, the teammates, and they can all sit happily in a park after. So I think it can get more people on bikes. It can be more than just seeing how fast you can go, it can be marketed in a fun sort of way. We're adding a fixed gear category to one race, for example."

Her plan for marketing that, at the moment, is that adding cyclocross into pre-existing festivals is a great way to get new people involved. "People are starting to understand that you can put on this race in a park, and they're looking at it as a thing they can add to their festivals. We need to keep partnering and growing, partnering and growing."

"How do you define cyclocross?" Wong asks, rhetorically. "Is it just for fun, since it is for 90% of the people? It's hard from a promoter's standpoint to decide who matters. In California, promoters don't like UCI races because it takes money away from the other categories."

When you do talk about the elite field in SoCal, Cameron believes that the racing scene in general in California is different. "You have so many pro road and mountain bike racers who live down there, so the 'cross scene is just so different. I've found there aren't as many people who are specialists in 'cross down there. Most of them are just fast road racers that are still fast cross racers, or pro mountain bikers who go do a cross race and beat everybody."

Wong agrees with this assessment, noting that racers in SoCal are likely to be from mountain biking, road racing, and even from motocross, or as she puts it, "strong guys from all disciplines." And while most of the racers are all into their other sports primarily, "That's why I love 'cross. It mixes up the tone because everyone is from another place but still come together."

The best part about having cyclocross in Los Angeles? "Seeing the downtown skyline of LA at night, lit up in the background, with a projection screen of the race and a crazy party going on, it's going to be sick. In a good way."

CROSSVEGAS

It's not a series, but CrossVegas is possibly the most well-known race in the US. It's also the world-wide unofficial "opener" of cyclocross season, and it's the brainchild of cyclocross devotee Brook Watts.

Back in the 70s, Watts got his first taste of promoting. He didn't mean for it to happen, but while racing, he says, "my station wagon became the registration center, it was carrying all the crap to races, and I was the go-to guy. Then it morphed into, 'Brook, can you help with this?' and they wanted to put on the '78 Nationals. My whole promotional background springs from that. My whole career is totally freaky."

After finding cyclocross in the 70s and helping organize one of the first Nationals as well as some bigger road racing, he departed from the world of race promotion for a few years. That's when he got real world, professional "discipline" working for a real ad agency, and those skills translated right back into cycling and promoting when he got downsized in 2004. "I went right back to the bike industry," he says. And he never looked back.

© Dejan Smaic

"My partner and I were so tired of going to Interbike [the biggest bicycle trade show in the country] and having nothing to do, so we said, 'What if we had a 'cross race at Interbike?' And boom. There's CrossVegas."

It was a whirlwind after that: "We flew out, we bought a city map at a gas station, went to every green spot on the map to see what would work, sat down with the parks department and convinced them that cyclocross was not a motorcycle event, signed a deal, and waited to see if anyone would show up."

The first year, people did show up and by Brook's recollection, there were about 4,000 spectators that Wednesday night. "The next day at

Interbike there were more orders for 'cross bikes than at any other time in the bike industry," he says. "I think it had a large impact on people in all four corners of the US saying, 'If they can do it in Vegas, we can do a 'cross race.'"

It ballooned even more in 2004 when Lance Armstrong made an appearance in the race. It was perfect timing too, because the race had gotten so big that Watts realized that they needed to fence in the park, in order to serve as crowd control. The event had gotten so good that it brought in too many spectators for the park and to the surrounding parking lots.

"From that point, it just took a big, big jump," Watts says. "It was kind of the benchmark. A couple years ago, it was obvious that CrossVegas had its own legs, when the crowd exceeded the Lance year—10,000 to 12,000 people were there. And those numbers aren't definite because you'll still see some fixie guy throwing his bike over the fence and climbing over, and it's like, 'More power to you.'"

Watts is now the proud promoter of the largest non-European 'cross race in the world. "By whatever measure you use, there's this great affinity for CrossVegas, it just seizes the imagination of people," he says.

While some promoters would consider having Lance Armstrong compete as the pinnacle of their race, Watts doesn't consider it his biggest coup. "Lance got us some legitimacy among non-'cross fans, but seeing pros like Lars Van Der Haar, Rob Peeters, and Bart Wellens." And if that makes him less patriotic towards American racers, so be it. "I want to see American 'cross racing develop," he says, and adds, "but when I see Europeans dominate the podium like they did last year, it's like, 'Wow, the race has arrived.' And that's a real neat sign."

For Watts, his best moment isn't planning the event, or looking at the press afterwards. "My best moment is once the race starts. I say 'Time Out.' The garbage can wait, the course marshals can wait, whatever crisis, can wait," he pauses, caught up in the memories. "Because I'm throwing a party right now and it's time for me to enjoy it. I climb up on stage, and I watch the freakin' race. And I go, 'Oh my God! Look at that move! I can't believe he did that!' I'm watching the race."

The future is bright for Watts, and he sees CrossVegas as an indicator that the sport is moving forward. "I'm real happy to see our sport grow," he says. "To move from 18 people on the start line at the 1978 Nationals to 100+ riders in CrossVegas, holy smokes! It's just incredible to see."

MID-ATLANTIC CYCLOCROSS SERIES

"The MAC is badass." –Jonny "El Gato" Sundt

"I trace the roots to New England to some extent, and that first class of elite racers were making runs up to New England and bringing it back to the Mid-Atlantic. I think that we developed our own culture, which is a little different than New England. We have a really strong racing scene and our races are really fierce and strong, but I think we still want to hang on to some of that grassroots, this-is-punk-rock kind of stuff, whereas New England is totally pro."

When you want to talk to one of the men behind the Mid-Atlantic Cyclocross Series, you talk to Marc Vettori. And he'll tell you he goes by Fat Marc, not Mr. Vettori. And in his words, "I'm not a guy who wins, and I don't have to win, but I like to fight. And as far as racing goes, I don't think there's any kind of racing where you have more fight going on than 'cross." The punk rock ethos he mentioned when talking about the Mid-Atlantic versus New England is quickly apparent as he talks about his feelings about cyclocross and the series that he's helped to create.

He didn't start the MAC series but he did quickly fall in love with it. Originally started by Andrew Albright, the MAC was started with the philosophy that "'cross shouldn't be at one high school, it should be at different venues, it should cover an area." And it grew from there. "Then there was the idea that we should set standards, payout-wise. Raise the money, set standards, attract better racers. Then it evolved with getting UCI races."

Now, the MAC encompasses a 14-race series in New Jersey, Pennsylvania, Maryland and Delaware. It's far enough south of New England that it has its own flavor, culture and local legends, but it's close enough that the top tier talent living in the Northeast still flocks down for the bigger races.

Fat Marc took on the eventual role in the MAC as "the guy with the big mouth who answers the questions. People hear who I am, see who I am." But aside from being the human megaphone, he's been behind the scenes as well: "I've been the scorekeeper for five years, my wife is on the board, I have my hand in five different MAC races."

It's truly a family affair, and the series director, Chris Auer, is actually the first elite men's champion of the series. Fat Marc credits the family-and-friends attitude to the overall vibe of the series. "The spirit of the MAC, the great racing and the people that come out, it's fun and people want to be a part of it."

The series started in 2005, and Fat Marc says, "The first growth I saw was when Nationals were in Providence. I think people who weren't racing 'cross had the chance to go to Nationals and saw it there, so for the Mid-Atlantic, it was our first big growth."

Since 2003, the series has grown into a behemoth, rivaling some of the New England races for participation, and stealing away racers with tempting prize purses and UCI points. The New England series directors and MAC directors work in tandem to develop a calendar that has as little UCI overlap as possible, to promote truly deep pools of talent in every event.

"If you want to race the best cyclocross in the Mid-Atlantic, you come to the MAC," Fat Marc says. "If you're a top ten guy in a local series, you might be top thirty in the MAC, and I think that's the lure. And the payouts are good, and that brings the best talent. It's consistent, you know what you're going to get, and you know you're going to have a good time."

Cyclocross in general has grown, and while the MAC appreciates the growth, Fat Marc has no illusions that we'll ever be like Europe. "I think it'll continue to get bigger because it's the most accessible kind of racing, and if you want to race, even if you're at the back of the pack, you're still battling. But it's participant-based and it's not in US culture, it's not in who we are, to be like they are in Europe."

But for the future of the MAC series, Fat Marc is a staunch believer in keeping it grassroots-based. "At the end of the day, cyclocross is a participant sport. The people who care about it are there. They want to see the races.

Fat Marc isn't hoping for major, commercial-grade growth. In fact, he knows how to bring in the money but opts to not make that push: "I know the money is in it if we can get the spectators, but I'm OK with not getting them." The races are often in areas that are harder for spectators to get to, like the beloved Granogue race in Delaware, where finding a restaurant post-race involves at least a 20 minute drive: not a site conducive to bringing in a big crowd. In addition, the MAC series is privately funded, unlike the Verge or Shimano series in New England. "I don't mind being part of a niche sport, something that's a little counter-culture."

The Mid-Atlantic region is another major hub of cyclocross, arguably due to the "trickle down" effect of the New England scene. Because the area is larger than the New England race scene, different series have developed. In addition to the MAC, there are several others in the area, including MABRA (Mid-Atlantic Bike Racing Association) Cross in the DC area. Initially, the series started by covering District 20: Northern Virginia, Maryland, DC, and Delaware. Bill Schieken, PR coordinator for the series, explains that, "Five years ago there were only ten races or so. Everything in the area was MABRA Cross and everyone is happy." However, he laughs, "Now, we're the victim of our own success and there are races cropping up everywhere. We went from having 14 races to having another series that has come off of it, and now we're at a point where MABRA Cross is just a generic term for any cyclocross race in the region."

Like the Hydra in Greek Mythology, cyclocross cannot be contained, and new races are cropping up each year. "There's the Super Eight series, which were the original MABRA Cross races. Plus, we always try to work with MAC so the races wouldn't conflict with each other, unless there was such a far distance between the two, like a race in New Jersey and one in Virginia."

While the races have increased, so have the racers, and Schieken is happy to say that, "It's gone from having fields of 20 people five years ago to having 1,000 racers at DCCX last year."

These professional series mean a lot to the elite racers who choose to travel large distances to race, and for some of them, the antics like beer—and dollar—handups tend to be distracting, and to some extent, take away from the professional levels of the racing. Ryan Trebon is one of those athletes, and says the reason for that is, "Our sponsors put out a lot of money to get us to these events like the USGP. I get kind of annoyed when guys show up and dick around, and they're doing dollar handups and beer feeds during the race and it's like, if you want to do that, there are tons of local races you can go do that."

For Trebon, he continues, "It's a serious race and we want to be taken seriously, not just by ourselves. If we want cyclocross to continue to grow, you have to limit that a little bit. It's OK to have fun but there's a time and a place for everything. When we're doing big races like Nationals or CrossVegas, it should be more professional."

So racers, take note, next time you're in one of the big series races, avoid taking the dollar feed, or offering it.

But when you're talking about big series, even though it isn't a UCI-designated series or a truly serious elite racer series, Oregon's Cross Crusades absolutely need to be mentioned.

CROSS CRUSADES

The promoters might focus on fun, but as Trebon reminds us, they put on a top quality event, even if it's not for the same reasons as other race promoters. "It's the most fun, but I also guarantee those guys are more dialed than 90% of all the promoters out there. They put on a good, quality event."

Cross Crusades is about the race, but almost more importantly, it's about the culture and overall party-atmosphere of the events. Molly Cameron elaborates: "It's really simple when I think about it. We just have this culture here in Portland that's a slacker culture. It's really easy to live here. It's kind of been this family thing, it's always been about being really inclusive and making it accessible for everybody."

And this is the goal: develop a local scene, not just focus on the top-level riders. Cameron says, "OBRA [Oregon Bicycle Racing Association] isn't looking to develop top riders. There are individuals within OBRA who do, but that's not what the mission statement is. We're not here to make pros that go on to be on pro tour teams. We just want to race our bikes and have fun. It's really easy to put on races. If you want to do it, you can make it happen. We have all the tools and equipment in place, it makes it easy for the racers and promoters."

Brad Ross is one of the promoters of the series, though he wasn't the original mastermind. "I sort of fell into promoting," he explains. "My two friends were the original promoters of the Crusade. At first I was just lending a hand. Then as the series grew, they both got busier with their 9-5 jobs. Since I was also promoting the Cascade Classic in the summer, it made sense for me to direct the Crusade too."

For Ross, he agrees with Cameron when he says that, "The most unique thing about the Crusade is that it is open and encouraging to anyone and everyone. We have taken a close look at what barriers keep newcomers from racing bikes and we do everything we possibly can to remove those barriers." The dedication to getting new racers into the scene is working, and Ross says that the race sees growth of 15% every year. "It's the biggest cross series in the world with average attendance in 2011 of 1,150 riders per day," he adds proudly.

The interesting part about that is that The Crusade doesn't do any formal marketing or advertising. "We just put on great races that people love to compete in," Ross says. "The Cross Crusade was started in 1993. But cross was alive and well here in Portland long before that."

The Cross Crusades are known nationwide, but when you take a look at the geographical profile, the races are all within a very small area, and none of them are UCI-designated, none of them fly in the big names. "This is it," Cameron says. "We have Portland. Everyone drives to Portland to race. It's just this crazy thing that snowballed. The first Cross Crusades that I did, they were still pretty big races, three or four hundred riders. I think beer has a lot to do with it, and the hanging out and the camaraderie. You can show up to this race, race for 45 minutes, and then be muddy and hang out with your buddies and have a good time."

Perhaps that lack of pretension in the scene is what draws people to it. "The promoter just cares about making people happy. He designs his courses so they're not necessarily spectator friendly but they are just racer-friendly. You have a good time." The Cross Crusades also differ from other series in one main way: the elite men and women all race together, though they are scored separately. And for most of the women, Cameron says, they enjoy this structure. "The elite women prefer racing with the men, and they race for the full hour. The ten women in the A race are really fast."

Since the start, the Crusades have kept growing, almost to the point where the growth has become a problem. "Since the Crusade has gotten so big, it has changed quite a bit from a logistical standpoint. Great venues that we used just ten years ago are now way too small. We require a minimum of eight acres just for parking. Our courses have gotten wider and less technical," Ross says. But the pros outweigh the cons: "At the same time, the whole festival atmosphere has taken off. I think 'cross is the best sport. I see it as a sport for men, women, and families of all ages and ability levels enjoying every fall. It could be huge."

"Portland has one million people and only 1,150 race cross each weekend in the fall. There should be five races going on here each with 1,150 riders. Why not? It's a blast."

EAST COAT VERSUS WEST COAST

Maybe the Cross Crusade series is somewhat indicative of the East Coast versus West Coast take on cyclocross racing in general. Trebon's opinon? "Guys in New England are just more serious in general. West Coast is a little more laid back, it's just a different mindset. It's not bad or good, just different. Races in New England, people are a little more stoic; West Coast people are more willing to just do whatever they want." Perhaps it's the laid back nature of the West Coast racers that create events more tailor-made to create a party atmosphere versus a more serious racing environment. It's not to say that West Coast racers don't ride hard, or that East Coast racers don't know how to party. They certainly do, on both counts. It's these different regional styles, however, that make racing in the US so interesting.

The East Coast wasn't always the more intense of the coasts though. Paul Curley remembers the early days of cyclocross in the US, and says, "The West Coast had a slightly different format that seemed more organized than what we had in New England." However, he's partially responsible for the shift. "I went over to Europe fairly early on, and tried to bring back some of the ideas that I got from over there. It's easier for people to go back and forth from Europe to the East Coast. It infiltrated into New England before it got to the West Coast."

In fact, the different regions having different styles of racing is similar to European cyclocross. Trebon says, "I think it's better to have a national scene, but even in Belgium, races are put on differently in different regions."

People have always argued where cyclocross came from in the US, and who began to build it into what it is today. However, those coastal tensions may be coming to an end, or at least, Mark Vareschi believes so. "There's less talk about the East or West Coast origins of cyclocross anymore," he says. "It's still regionalized, but I wonder if there's a connection between the explosion of social media and the nationalization of the sport, along with the lessening of tensions between the East Coast and West Coast. It's silly, but it's true. I'm just glad we're not fighting over who invented American cyclocross anymore."

The scenes did develop differently from region to region. Kat Statman suggests that the development was infinitely different than in Europe, for different reasons that varied from coast to coast. "Seeing the Euro development of it as 'we need training for the winter,' compared to cyclocross in the US," he says, is different, "because we adopted it so much later, the West Coast sort of adopted it as this weird joke, almost what's happening on the East Coast with alleycats [bike messenger unofficial races]."

As a West Coast elite racer, Molly Cameron has a slightly more outspoken opinion than Trebon on the East Coast versus West Coast scenes.

"Attitude-wise? The East Coast definitely thinks it's the shit. I envy the East Coast a little. In Portland, people want to race bikes but they don't want to put a lot into it on the West Coast. It's almost frowned upon if you're really serious. On the East Coast, people are bike racers."

This serious attitude, Cameron argues, can be a pro or a con. "The majority of races out there, people aren't going to party and drink beer, they're going there to race their bike. And some people have fun racing their bikes and some people take it really seriously, or way too seriously."

On the West Coast, it's possible to take racing seriously without maybe the same serious attitude that the East Coast seems to have. "The scene we have here now didn't develop because of bike racers, it developed because of fans. All of our fans are riders, so the genius thing is getting people to come to the race, and then they're all going to hang out so you have 1,000 fans at any given time watching the race."

Andrew Yee has an interesting perspective, having raced in New England for a decade and then relocating to the West Coast. He agrees with Cameron, saying, "I've always felt like the West Coast is more about participation and partying, and the East Coast, perhaps because it seems to attract a greater percentage of roadies, was more focused on racing accomplishments. I believe that over the last five or ten years, that's started to change even on the East Coast, and you'll see examples like Gloucester being sponsored by a brewery, now there are beer tents and it's a big part of the culture, but something about the West Coast and laid back nature and lifestyle makes it more focused on the party."

Yee makes a great point though: the practicality of the party atmosphere on the West Coast just makes more sense. "Part of the attitude has to be chalked up to the fact that half the season in New England is in frigid, frozen, bitter cold conditions, and it's much harder to sit around and barbecue and drink beer when it's 30 degrees out and snowing. I've tried to do it and we've done it, and it's hard. On the West Coast, you attract the crazies like me, but also the weekend warrior and he's much more likely to hang around."

He also believes that part of it is based on where racers in cyclocross come from, in terms of their sport backgrounds. "If you look at early West Coast dudes, they're mostly mountain bikers like Don Myrah," Yee says. "Then you look at New England guys, and those guys are without a doubt road racers."

And Vareschi also adds, "New Englanders approach life differently and cyclocross becomes this performance or ritual that enacts all of those things, that day-to-day are just part and parcel. Everything we do in the Northeast is kind of intense and I think that plays out in the race scene and how the series are run. It's not just about cyclocross, it's about the relationship between the sport and culture."

Unlike the European scene, which tends to be more nationalistic and fans tend to be rooting for one or two racers specifically, Trebon points out that, "Here, we're all fans of cycling. They don't hate Tim and Jeremy on the West Coast, they don't hate me on the East Coast. It's great to mix it up." And maybe that's why, in his opinion, "I think a lot of riders want to come here because of the mellow atmosphere and because it's more fun."

Of course, there are plenty of other areas where cyclocross has taken root. The Midwest has a burgeoning scene, Wisconsin, Illinois and Ohio are rapidly filling their race calendars, and Texas cyclocross (TXCX) has grown in leaps and bounds. The southern part of the East Coast isn't without a scene either: Georgia and Florida both have series running, and North Carolina will be hosting Nationals in 2015. And just inside the West Coast, there's Colorado, home of the Boulder Cup series as well as the famous Wednesday Night Worlds.

"The growth of the Colorado cross scene over the past 20 years has been stunning," Pete Webber explains. "A lot of people have made it happen, but two names stand out: Chris Grealish and Brian Hludzinski. These guys have put on races forever and created some of our biggest events and series. Without race promoters willing to endure the difficulties of organizing races, 'cross wouldn't happen. One of the best things we have going is the Wednesday Worlds in Boulder. It's been going for nearly 20 years and has grown to 50 or 60 riders every week. It has introduced a ton of people to 'cross."

And in every part of the country, race series are starting to work on finding a mass appeal. "There's a transition to family-friendly," Webber says. "It's great to see parents and kids racing in their age groups in the morning, and then cheering at the elite race."

The question still remains: would it be better for the US to develop a more national scene, versus the regional scenes it currently has? Some believe that a more cookie cutter style of races would be better, because it would hold all races to the same standards. However, to do that would be taking away the regional flair that makes each series unique in its own right. Cameron thinks that a blend of the regional quirks would do the US cyclocross scene a world of good. "If the growth of it was perfect, we would mix the East and West Coast scenes," she says. "We'd have Cross Crusades style races on the East Coast with a really top notch Elite field and UCI presentation, and the same thing on the West Coast. We'd still have the Crusades but we'd be able to have really top level fields at every race."

MEET A PROMOTER: Murphy Mack

California is one of the original hubs of cyclocross in the US, and while it may not have the UCI prestige that New England has anymore, it still hosts a large amount of races, UCI and otherwise. People like Murphy Mack and Dorothy Wong are tasked with making sure every event runs smoothly, from the craziness that was SingleSpeed World Championships to the more professional and serious LACX Series.

Murphy Mack hasn't been around for too long, but he's already become a staple of California racing. "I've been helping out with the Lion of Fairfax CX race here in the Bay Area for about five years now. It's in its sixth year this fall. It's widely regarded as 'the mountain biker's 'cross race' due to the terrain it's held on. The race I created, Stafford Lake CX, also in Marin County, is returning for a second year this fall. The course layout is super rad and we put in some barriers of unusual size that the racers really love."

Why so varied? "We're staying within the rules but not showing racers the same old thing they see everywhere else. I've had no less than six people tell me it was their favorite race of the year last year. Hearing feedback like that is what drives me and makes me feel that I'm really on the right track."

As a promoter, Mack has a more unique view of the growth of the racing scene in the past few years: after all, to him, growth translates into profit that a race brings in. He says, "The main thing I've seen is a few growth spurts. Now that cycling in general is getting bigger from the groundswell of urban riders (mostly commuters and fixed gear riders), I'm seeing yet another expansion of the ranks. I think a good number of the new racers are younger people who maybe started riding when their friends got them into riding fixed and now they're starting to want to branch out into other disciplines of the sport. I see a lot of them getting into cyclocross."

But as far as spectator growth is concerned, it's slow going. But Mack is making a push, first by trying to keep a crowd as opposed to drawing one. "I pull in solid crowds by offering a race that's going to be as difficult as it is fun. Three or four short, easy, uneventful flat laps is boring. We race cyclocross because it's hard. I try to offer a challenging, fun race that is part of a package of not just the race, but also food and a beer tent if possible too. It's supposed to be racing and spectating. Not just racing and then run to your car to go home. I really believe in the concept of a hard race and a good time. If you want easy, stay home and sit on the couch and take bong hits while you play video games."

But as far as actually getting non-racing, non-family spectators interested, Mack doesn't think cyclocross in the US is quite at that point yet, though he's willing to make a push for it. "I think the number of spectators is somewhat dependent upon the venue. If you're close to a major metropolitan area, you're going to see more spectators than if you're at some out-of-the-way venue. Reaching out to the public to get more spectators is something we're just going to do for the first time this year."

He concludes by saying, "The racers who do this deserve to have some fans."

RICHARD FRIES REVEALS HIS ANNOUNCING SECRETS

© Pedal Power Photography

Want to be an announcer? It's not as easy as you might think. Every race has a story, and it's up to the announcer to not only make the crowd know about the story, the announcer's job is to make the crowd care about it as well. And if there's one announcer who exemplifies electrifying the crowd, it's Richard Fries. "The entire SuperCup series came down to that race. Every storyline that you can imagine was there. It was the young rookie taking on the jaded old pro, it was Darth Vader in the evil empire versus Luke Skywalker, and when Mark Gullickson attacked on the final run-up, it was the loudest roar that many people could have ever made. It was how the course was, how the visuals were, the sound was perfect."

HIS TOP TIPS

1. At that race, I didn't have a wireless mic because it wouldn't

work there, so at night we dug a trench from the main stage and we laid cable in this trench through an electrical transformer box, and I spent the time standing on this box the size of my desk. Because to announce, you have to take the high ground, and that's the biggest mistake that announcers make: to sit on a stage in a 'cross race, because you can't see anything.

2. If I've done one thing well, it's that I'll find a place where I can look within inches of a rider and his bike. I can see which tires are rolling, I can see if he's in the big ring or little ring, I can see mud clearance, tire pressure, change of tires.

3. The other important thing as an announcer is the ability to run into the pits and get information from the mechanics. That's an awesome talking point.

Tips From Promoters

"Don't be afraid to delegate and surround yourself with great people."   —Fat Marc Vettori, MAC Series

"You have to be passionate because you work your ass off. It's like being an entrepreneur. But if you're working your ass off for what you're passionate about, then life is good."   —Dorothy Wong

"The best tip? 'Don't do it' is definitely my best tip. I've been very lucky that people do appreciate what I do, people are beginning to understand how hard it is to put these on, and they understand how much I care about these races. But it's just a lousy job. I don't know anyone who likes it. We all love our finished product, we love what we achieved. But as for advice? Start small, go slow. Focus on quality. Don't try to do everything at once."   —Adam Myerson

"The top pro racers are smart. They know it's not just about the prize money. It's about what kind of exposure they're going to get if they go to a race, and they know we've built it so they know the racing is going to be good, the course is going to be good, the experience is going to be quality. As a result of us putting that work and effort into the race, it makes it eligible to be a C1 [Class 1-the highest UCI ranking for races that are not World Cups or championship races], and by virtue of working really hard to produce a good race, we're going to attract the top pros. They'll have crowds to race in front of. It's a combination of everything. We try to be very consistent to our sponsors, with what we deliver to our sponsors."

–Joan Hanscom

"You can't preach to the choir. Use the 80-20 rule about getting racers. Do your job about getting the word out to racers, among the cycling community, but you have to take a page from every other promotion that's done in the world. Create a compelling story as to why someone should give up their free time to come out and enjoy this event."

–Brook Watts

"An average Crusade race is way bigger and more raucous than all but the very biggest UCI races in the US. My tip to other promoters is don't let yourself get hamstrung by rules and regulations. The Cross Crusade answers to no one except our customers."

–Brad Ross

Often, promoters assume that they know what racers want on a course, and at a race. But it's not always so simple. Some of the elite racers have some tips for promoters looking to grow their series.

Laura Van Gilder's advice to promoters is simple: "They have the potential to make it big in the US because it's such an accessible sport. It's very spectator-friendly, it's accessible to youth, and if we can have the foresight to focus on that, instead of if we just worry about growing the top end of it, it will grow. Make all the races good, don't just cater to the elite."

5: ELITE MEN IN US CYCLOCROSS

"I'm planning on being good." –Ryan Trebon

You can't talk about cyclocross without a (pun intended) cross-sampling of the elite fields. They're broken into three main groups: elite men, juniors and Under-23 racers, and elite women. As with any sport that hasn't quite made it to the "big leagues" in the US, it's hard to classify who elite racers are, and who the big names are. In any given region, there are local heroes, the men and women that dominate the series that occupy the area. However, there are several noteworthy personalities and racers in the sport, and their stories of how they came to race 'cross are interesting indeed. The best way to gain insight into the sport is to see how the racers came to be involved in it and how they came to love it.

If you already know a bit about racing road bikes or mountain bikes, you know that the racers in those sports do it because of love for the sport, but it's arguably more true in cyclocross. Many of the pro racers in the sport are pro road or mountain bike racers in their own right, who either choose to sacrifice their free time during the off-season to race 'cross, or quit their other sport altogether in order to devote more time to cyclocross.

There are too many top level elite racers in the US to possibly fit them into one volume, so consider this a random sampling of some of the better known racers and characters that populate the scene.

Jeremy Powers

The latest National Champion, Jeremy Powers has finally achieved the dream that's managed to elude him for years. In 2010, spectators and reporters watching felt their hearts break for the 28-year-old racer as he crashed spectacularly at Nationals and lost his chance at the title. In 2012, the following season, the crowd went wild when Powers flew off the front at the end of the race, holding off the chase group as he made his way into the finishing straight for the win, crying with happiness. This glimmer of emotion in the racer is uncharacteristic: Powers is best known as the smiling, goofy racer responsible for the sport's first "reality show," *Behind THE Barriers,* filmed by Sam Smith.

© Dejan Smaic

Powers's talent as both a racer and a personality within the sport make him one of the most interesting elite racers in the US. "He's really putting down some tracks for others to come up and race in this country in cyclocross," Geoff Proctor says. "These guys are finally starting to make a living based on their cyclocross, not on the road and not on mountain bikes, and I hope to see that continue."

It almost didn't happen though. "I started out racing as a junior when I was 13 years old with mountain biking. My mom took me to my first mountain bike race and she said that 'we're never doing this again.' Because I dropped out of the first three mountain bike races that I did. Dropped out because I was on a 24-inch wheel Giant Awesome mountain bike. That's the true name of it."

Powers continued, rushing through his words like he still was the nervous boy he was remembering: "I wasn't familiar with the scene and nervous and didn't like not knowing where I was, being alone in the woods, just a super nervous 13-year-old racing mountain bikes for the first time. I had a rigid bike, the wheels weren't big enough to go over anything so I would keep flying over the handlebars, so I dropped out. And the last time I dropped out, she said we were never going to another bike race again because we were wasting my time and her time."

His mom, thankfully, eventually forgave the errant Powers, but her words stuck in his mind. "I remembered my mom telling me I needed to do well, or at least show some want or desire. So after she said that, I kept riding all the time, and she bought me another bike that Christmas and put it under the tree. It was a Specialized Stumpjumper with a Mag 21 shock and I remember just loving it. It was the coolest thing."

And so it began. "That year I raced a bunch and had some decent results in mountain biking. Tom Masterson was coaching me at the time and he was saying that cyclocross was a great way to stay in shape for mountain biking, so I started doing cyclocross on my mountain bike and I remember doing my first race on my mountain bike, and then the tires were too slow so I did my second race on my road bike with 28 mm 'cross tires."

Powers gradually began the shift from mountain biking to cyclocross, saying, "I did it every winter after that, a little more serious. Then in 2000, I got fourth at Nationals and qualified to go to Worlds in the Czech Republic, and I got to race at Worlds. I was sixteen. My dad came and watched, I jumped the barriers and people still talk about that."

He paused to add, "Yeah, I've been jumping the barriers for a hot minute."

He sums up his start simply by saying, "So that's how I got into 'cross racing. I needed to do it to stay fit but I saw I was decent about it, and then when I was 16 and started to get decent results, that's when I started focusing on it."

After that first World Championship, he started working with Adam Myerson as his coach, and traveled to the Supercup races, which were the equivalent of today's USGP series. And in New England, Powers learned to be a real racer: "I'd be racing in the 35+ field, so I was racing with Paul Curley and guys that were really good and they taught us everything. That's how we learned all the dirty tricks like how to put someone into a corner, New England style."

As a junior racer, he won his first Nationals race in Providence, Rhode Island. He says, "That was my breakout, my last year as a junior. Then the next year, I focused on road and cyclocross, switched away from mountain biking."

And as his 'cross career progressed, he started to switch to even skinnier tires. "On the road, that year, I went from a Cat 3 to a 1 that season and got signed by Jelly Belly in 2004 after racing for the Northampton Cycling Club for two years." But luckily, unlike some racers who abandoned 'cross for a career on the road, Powers remained firmly committed to making it as a 'cross racer.

Perhaps the reason he was able to stay in cyclocross and have it be a viable career option was his location: as a New Englander, he was surrounded by the men and women who had been in the sport since early on, including Stu Thorne, the founder of CyclocrossWorld.com. Powers says, "I started to do the USGPs and had success. I got on the podium three or four times. I made a decent impression. Then, in 2007, I started with Cyclocrossworld.com, and that's where I realized that US cyclocross was actually taking off. And Stu Thorne really helped launch my career in cyclocross then."

It was good timing too. Powers reflects, "Cyclocross really has continued to grow and take off here. The series has gotten bigger, more sponsors have come in and every year I've been able to make more money racing."

But for Powers, no title will mean as much as the 2012 Elite Men's National Title did. "It feels great," he says, "Every time I have the jersey on I have a lot of pride. I worked super hard for this goal I wanted to accomplish, and it took me a long time to get it. I'm excited to wear that jersey and have that title because it's something that eluded me for so long and I finally have it. I don't have to describe myself as someone who's been a good rider but never gotten that title, which is something that's plagued me for a long time. It means a lot.

Tim Johnson

The first racer from the United States to capture a place on a Worlds podium, Tim Johnson has had one of the longest, most successful careers in cyclocross in the US. At 35 years old, he's one of the older elite racers, but his career is far from finished.

Pete Webber: "Here, Tim Johnson takes the win at the Boulder Cup race, set against some of the greatest landscape that the US has to offer."
© Dejan Smaic

Tim wasn't always a cyclocross racer. Like most other pro cyclocross racers in the US, he started as a mountain biker, and eventually shifted more towards a focus on cyclocross, as it became a more viable career option. "I did MTB worlds in September of '95 as a junior. I got home, I had taken a month and traveled around Europe by myself. Got home, basically left my MTB boxed up and went to the shop and Stu was like, 'What are you going to do now?' and I didn't have an answer for him."

Tim paused and continued. "I had no idea. I had graduated high school and was taking the year off before college and he was like, well, let's go do a 'cross race. We jumped in his giant station wagon and I don't even know what I got, fourth or fifth. I had a blast. I had no idea what I was doing, I was bunnyhopping some of the stuff, and then I just loved it. A couple weeks later, I got a cross bike I could actually use. Then we had Nationals there, at home in Western Massachusetts."

It took a while for cyclocross to take off as a sport, and for Tim to start being noticed for his skills, but when it did happen, in true Tim Johnson fashion, it led to a great story. "When I was working in REI at the time of Nationals, and I kept calling in sick so I could go to cross races. I tried to get off the day of junior 'cross Nats and they said no. That was when Nationals was one day. I wanted the day off but they wouldn't give it to me, so I was like, 'Well, I'll just call in sick.' So I went ahead, called out sick, went and raced Nationals, and I got second but I ended up getting the title because of the junior roll-out thing. On Monday, I get a phone call from my boss, and she's like, 'You know what? Don't bother coming in, I'll send a paycheck to your house.' So I'm like, 'Great, awesome, I just got fired.' A month later, I went back into the store and went to a magazine that had my picture on the cover, and was like, 'thanks, guys.' It was on the newsstand. For sale. So, 'Thanks for the understanding.'"

He won that year at Nationals, unsurprisingly, and he continued to improve and impress. After winning Nationals, he found himself being crowned the first ever American to make it onto a Worlds podium, that year as an Under-23 racer.

Since then, Johnson's star has been on the rise. With multiple National Championships and as the first US racer to snag a spot on a podium at World Championships, Johnson is the Golden Child of cyclocross, its first grand experiment in US success.

Ryan Trebon

Like most racers who started in other cycling disciplines, Trebon is by no means sure of where or when exactly he caught the cyclocross bug. All he knows is that it happened, and he fell in love with the sport fast. "I don't remember exactly, but it was probably 2003," he explains. "I was mostly racing mountain bikes and I just started racing for fun on my mountain bike. I did one year like that and got a proper cyclocross bike the year after that."

While some of the New England racers started immediately in UCI fields because that was what was available, pros like Trebon who didn't live on the East Coast started locally. But the races were hard, and he had no choice but to jump right into the already burgeoning pro field. "I started racing in the pro race, not in UCI races but just local ones: if you race professional mountain bikes, they make you race professional cyclocross. Then I started doing well, so I started racing more and I started taking it more seriously and making it more of a priority."

The racing led to a team, though mountain bikes were still a priority as he began to race for Kona. "I first started racing for Kona in 2004 and the majority of what they wanted was mountain bikes but then Barry and I started doing really well with cyclocross, so I decided that was what I really wanted to focus on."

"So 2005 was when I started shifting my focus," he says, "and now it's 100% cyclocross and I just do road and mountain to supplement it."

And success followed. Despite Trebon's talent on the mountain bike, his heart was in the right place once he discovered cyclocross. "I won national championships on mountain bike, but I just liked cyclocross more. I like the racing better, and I think it's definitely bigger in the US than mountain bike stuff is. It's just not there, you know? People don't care about it as much. I like that people are passionate about cyclocross, and fans come out and cheer. There's a strong national circuit.

© Dejan Smaic

"I really like Ryan Trebon a lot, and a lot of people see him on a day when something breaks and he's frustrated. He's a very emotional rider," announcer Richard Fries says, adding, "And that's what makes him a really great rider. He's one of the most intense guys on race day—but holy shit, it's an intense sport."

Since his long stint with Kona—seven years—Trebon has made some changes. As he says, "That's a long time to stay with one program." But he was happy there, despite his desire to do something different. "They were awesome, really supportive. But we wanted to do something else last year, but we weren't really making any money doing it the way we tried. It was a test drive." Trebon started his own team with the combination of LTS and Felt, and raced essentially solo in the 2011 season. Since then, he's signed on to the powerhouse that is Cannondale-CylocrossWorld.com and is already raring to go for the 2012 season.

He's had plenty of success domestically with two wins at US Nationals as an elite man, as well as a four time USGP series winner. But his arguably most impressive results come from overseas, with a fifteenth place at Worlds, and top tens at several World Cups and Super Prestige races. His favorite? "Winning Nationals is always nice. But that World Cup in 2007 in Hoogerheide. It was the worst possible weather, 37 degrees, half snow, half sleet, freezing. It was a hard race, lots of people were dropping out because it was just too cold. It was a good result because it was just hard. There was nothing easy about it."

There isn't anything easy about cyclocross in general, but it's the intense love of the sport that keeps pros like Trebon coming back for more.

His favorite moment in racing came on US soil, despite the fact that he's arguably prouder of his across-the-pond results. "I remember winning Nationals in Bend and it was really noisy. Almost too noisy. On top of the stair flyover it was just obscenely loud. Just too loud. I couldn't hear, I couldn't concentrate, but that was one of my favorite moments."

Adam Myerson

"I heard about Adam when I found an interview he did where he talked about skinhead culture and scooters and veganism and cyclocross. And I thought, 'he seems like an interesting guy and I'd like to meet him.'"
—Mark Vareschi

A cornerstone of cyclocross in New England, Adam Myerson has been racing 'cross since 1989. In addition to being an elite racer, he's one of the founding fathers of cyclocross in New England today, and was responsible for what eventually evolved into the Verge and Shimano Series. He's also one of the longest running elite riders in the US, since he's been racing in the pro field for over 20 years.

As a native New Englander, cyclocross was always in the cards for Myerson, as soon as he started racing for the Mass Bay Road Club when he was a junior. "That was the club that Tom Stevens, Paul Curley, Mark and Frank McCormack, basically the heart and soul of New England cyclocross, rode for. So I got introduced to 'cross and it was more or less peer pressure, it was just what you did. If you were on this team, of course you were going to race 'cross."

© Pedal Power Photography

When he started racing, there was no junior race for him to jump into, and no prize for being the top Under 23 rider in a race. In fact, there wasn't much structure to cyclocross at all. He says, "When I started and was first doing well, there was no such thing as an Under 23 category. There was no Super Cup, no National series, and the Worlds team was very unsupported."

That makes asking him about his earlier successes nearly impossible, since as he says, "When I look back at results, I see that I was the first Under 23 in all of these races, so it's hard to quantify the earlier results in my career. If you got a top 10 in races in New England in the 90s as a 22-year-old, that's actually a pretty spectacular result if you translate it to modern times."

As a racer at the University of Massachusetts in Amherst, Myerson helped to "pioneer" cyclocross in the Pioneer Valley, now home to racers like Jeremy Powers and Justin Lindine. It was also a collegiate race that led him to one of his best early results: winning collegiate Nationals in Denver in 1997. "It was my last year of school, Tim Johnson was second, and if you look at the rest of the field—Tom Danielson, Alex Candelario—it's a good top ten. It's all guys who went on to do something," he says, adding somewhat ruefully, "I didn't get much better after that but a lot of those guys did."

His star power increased over the years, especially with the advent of social media [see Cyclocross Hijinks chapter], but it wasn't until many years later that he took the win in a UCI race, and it meant the world to him. "When I finally won my first UCI race at Downeast, that should have happened years before but for one reason or another, it didn't, so when I finally put it all together and won, and then again later that season, that was really special and important to me, personally."

"Adam walks the walk and I think in many ways he's responsible for the way we think and talk about cyclocross, at least in its contemporary form," Vareschi says, and he's right. When asked about influential people in cyclocross, most of the racers, both young and old, interviewed have pointed back to Myerson.

As a racer, team manager and promoter, something eventually had to give, and Myerson has recently let go of the reins of the Verge and Shimano Series in New England. But in 2010, he said a final goodbye in a fashion that was as meaningful for the crowd as it was for him: by winning the overall Verge Series in the Elite Men's category. "Winning that series was big for me. Since the series was suspended the next year, it felt like the end of the chapter and it was a really good way to close it."

Geoff Kabush

While Geoff Kabush may not be technically an American cyclocross rider (he's Canadian), he chooses to race cyclocross almost exclusively in the US, focusing primarily on the USGP series as a way to stay in shape in his off-season. As a pro mountain biker during the spring and summer, he's on an abbreviated 'cross schedule, but that hasn't stopped the man with the muttonchops from being one of the top racers in the USGP series, taking second to Jeremy Powers in 2011.

Kabush isn't new to cyclocross, though he's steadily gotten more serious over the years, as the competition grew stiffer. "Growing up in British Columbia, I was a mountain biker first, for sure. Then I lived in Vancouver and rode with one teammate who was into 'cross a bit, and that's when the Supercup series was going on, back in 1997. Seattle had a pretty big 'cross scene, so I went down for a Supercup weekend, and it was similar to the USGP today. It was a really cool event and I had a fun weekend there."

Kabush wasn't all about the fun though. "For sure the first year I did the USGP series in 2004, I had some really good battles with the Twin Towers [Trebon and Wicks, the two tallest elite racers, both of whom were riding for Kona at the time]." All of Kabush's major victories have happened in the USGPs, though he's never taken the overall series title. "Winning the USGP at Gloucester was definitely one of my bigger victories. I lost that overall series that year by two points to Wicks."

Now, Kabush says, "We have some kind of base in the US so whenever I've done it I've focused on the USGP series, because it's the biggest and funnest racing in North America."

However, it's not all fun and games for Kabush, at least not anymore. 'Cross has grown in leaps and bounds, and the level of talent in the pro field has grown to match it. "Several years later, I started doing a little more. When I switched from Kona to Maxxis in 2004, that's when the USGP series was getting a bit of momentum and that was the first year I had the support to do the whole USGP series. It was a bit more relaxed back then. Not that it's not fun now, but we could cruise through the series and really enjoy the atmosphere and 'cross camaraderie, and since then, most winters I've done at least some of the USGPs."

© Dejan Smaic

Despite the fact that Kabush is feeling the pressure in the behemoth that is the USGP series, he has no intention of switching to local racing instead. For him, "the USGP is great because it goes to the start of December, so I get a break before mountain bike training starts. Unfortunately, there aren't enough months in the year, because I'd love to take a trip to Europe and do World Championships sometime, but it's tough since my job is being a mountain biker."

Molly Cameron

"I take every race so seriously, whether I win or lose. I'm up one weekend and the next, I'm just devastated. I try to have this soldier mentality about that, where I just race bikes and this is what I do, so I do it as best as I can every time. It almost doesn't matter if I win or lose, it's just my job. I go and I race. And it's emotional."

© Dejan Smaic

Cameron is one of the main "personalities" in cyclocross. An elite racer for the past eight years, Cameron has shifted focus from a global racing season to a more local one, racing in the Cross Crusades in Portland, Oregon. However, Cameron is still one of the more adventurous US elite racers, leading the charge over to Japan when a UCI race was announced there in 2011.

Cameron discovered cyclocross in 2004 after a move to Oregon. While she (Cameron is transgendered) began by racing on the track, a holdover from her time as a bike messenger and track racer in the Bay Area, by 2000, she had decided she didn't want to race anymore. But in Oregon, Cameron says, "the scene was so much easier and more fun and inclusive and it's super accessible here, to just race your bike. I started racing the track a little, and one summer, they told me there was a cyclocross race, and I was like, 'Oh, what's cyclocross?'" As with many of the other pros, it only took one race. Lucky for Cameron, that first race was Alpenrose, which was at the velodrome where Cameron had been racing. She says, "I did a little research and realized, 'Whoa, this sounds really cool.' And that was one of my first races, the Cross Crusade at Alpenrose." Despite racing for a few years prior, compared to most of the locals, Cameron felt like the newbie. "You talk about West Coast 'cross and you're talking about people who've been racing for a really long time," she says. But she persevered, making trips to the East Coast to race in the bigger UCI races. While 2004 is only a few years ago, Cameron got started before 'cross began to really take off. "It's gotten deeper," she says. "Maybe four or five years after my first cross race, I was a pretty fast single-speeder, and I won the Cross Crusades single-speed series in 2004 and 2005. The next year, I wanted a bigger challenge so I figured I'd get a geared bike and race the elite category. But in the last five or six years of racing, the talent has just gotten deeper."

At that point, "the races were really small and the fields weren't super deep." Cameron's memories of early USGPs involved small, but deep, fields: "I remember one of the Sun Prairie USGPs, Jon Page was there, Brian Matter, Tim Johnson and Todd Wells. So there were four top pros, and then a dozen—I call them—B-Tier guys. The lower-tier riders, where we're fighting for scraps."

"I could go to a UCI race and top 10," Cameron remembers. "Then a few years later, there were a dozen guys who were all fighting for fourth through tenth."

She isn't unhappy about the shift though. Rather, she believes it raises the level for everyone. "I used to be able to travel all over the US and really fight for UCI points, and now, it's pretty rad because I can't show up and fake it. I have to be on my A game at every race, even the crappiest little UCI races."

Despite the changing fields, Cameron was one of the first elite racers to focus on 'cross, though her reasoning was primarily based on wanting to focus her business at the Portland Bicycle Studio. She concludes, "Now you go and there are so many strong riders coming to 'cross from all sorts of disciplines and it's getting more specialized. People like me, I only race 'cross now."

Todd Wells

While Todd Wells is best known for his prowess as a mountain bike racer, to say that he's also a great 'cross racer is an understatement. Because of his mountain biking commitments, he doesn't often toe the line at races during the season, but when he does, the other pros can expect a hard fight to stay in front—or close behind—him. Most recently, he took the National title for the third time.

As with many of the other mountain-bikers-turned-cyclocrossers, Wells' career started on a 'cross course with a mountain bike … with one minor difference. "The first CX race I ever did was the Super Cup at an Army base outside of Boston back in 1997 I think. I was racing mountain bikes and the Super Cup was a pretty big deal, the top riders used to get called up out of smoking circus tents. I modified a MTB with drop bars for the race."

However, the first race didn't immediately lead to amazing results, though it did lead to a love of the sport. I think both Marc Gullickson and the McCormack brothers all lapped me. But I just thought cyclocross bikes looked so cool, the hybrid between road and MTB, I couldn't wait to get one of those bikes."

From there though, Wells' cyclocross star was on the rise. He took his first National title in Maryland in 2001. It would be four years before he took his second title in Providence, leading him to a deep appreciation for the wins. "They seem to come in spaced out intervals. Just as I seem to be dropping out of the conversation of potential winners, I managed to pull something out. I think my victory in Rhode Island was my favorite because it was such horrible conditions, snowy, muddy, cold and everything we think of when we think cyclocross."

© Dejan Smaic

As a racer primarily focused on mountain biking, there are tradeoffs for Wells, especially as the cyclocross scene in the US develops its own focused racers. He says, "It is becoming harder and harder as CX gains momentum in the US. It used to be a training tool for the MTB. No one took it too seriously and no one even started to think about it until road or MTB season was over. I used to be able to do some fun training and still hope to be competitive enough to win a few races."

But now, it's a whole different ballgame. People like Johnson and Powers shifting to a 'cross-focus has, according to Wells, "lifted the level of the sport quite a bit in the US and requires devoted specific training to be competitive. It wasn't long ago that the McCormacks were the only US riders going to the World Championships and they would get lapped. Now we have riders getting medals and popping top-10s in the World Cups."

Wells won't be hanging up the skinny tires anytime soon though. Despite the difficulties of racing 'cross, especially in an Olympic year as a mountain biker, Wells says, "I love racing 'cross." Of course, loving something doesn't make it easy, and he adds, "I feel that now I have to really pick and choose which races I want to try and do well in. That limits the amount of races I get to do and makes the season more stressful. It requires well planned breaks and a lot of mental energy to be competitive all year."

But despite the exhaustion that comes from racing two disciplines, nearly year round, Wells loves cyclocross. "My favorite part about 'cross racing is the camaraderie, atmosphere and group racing. It's great to see the road and 'cross guys who I don't get to see all year on the MTB circuit in the fall." And despite its growing professionalism, he says, "You still have people dressing up in costumes and having a lot of fun out there though, it has a festival type of feel which I really enjoy."

Wells' last note about why he loves cyclocross is simple: he's got a need for speed. "I love racing in a group at high speed. I don't get that much on the MTB so it is so much fun to be elbow-to-elbow chasing down moves and attacking. You can't lose focus for a second or you'll make a mistake and have a crash, lose the group or just get out of your rhythm. It's an amazing sport."

Jonathan Page

"I would stand on a mountaintop and say Jonathan Page deserves more attention," Brook Watts claims. And he's arguably right. Page has been a staple of American cyclocross for years, however, he's one of the few Americans who focuses on racing in Europe.

He's also the only American elite man to make it onto the podium at the World Championships. "That was a fun day," he says laconically, the New Englander in him creeping out. "It didn't strike me as out of the ordinary, I just had a very good day. I had injured my shoulder in October and ruined it, ripped the two major tendons off of my bones. I was at the lowest you can think of. My wife, Cori, and I, we didn't turn on the heat in our house because we had no money because I wasn't racing or getting start money or having prize money coming in. It made me tougher."

He was under doctor's orders to take at least three months off the bike, but by December he was racing again and, as he puts it, getting better and better as he "trained and trained and trained." He made it onto the podium in Providence at Nationals, and then went on to snag Bronze at Worlds a month later. "I was just happy to be at the front of the race," he remembers. "I didn't know I was leading the race at any point. I started in the last row, I didn't have any UCI points. It was a whirlwind. Now, I'd like to do it again."

Despite being one of the older elite racers at 36 years old, Page still is making waves. Until recently, he lived in Belgium year-round, and only returned stateside for one race last year: Nationals, where he took third place, bringing his total to three wins at Nationals and seven total podium finishes.

"I'd say that all of my National Championships wins are special," Page says. "I've gotten podiums in SuperPrestige races and races like that too. But what's really cool is that it doesn't matter what the event is, when my kids are there and cheering, that's special for me."

He hasn't always been the dad on the course though: he started racing at 16 in New England. "I've been racing since I was a junior: I started way back when!" he explains. "I used to race all over the US. But 10 years ago we started living in Belgium, and before that we were in Germany for a bit and then Switzerland a few years before that. It was only for a couple months at a time at first." The actual move to Belgium came when, Page says, "I figured I might as well try to race with the best in the world, so that's what I decided to do."

Racing with the top Europeans is unlike racing in the US, and Page found that he preferred the Euro mode of racing. "There, they just get the most out of themselves and out of the race," he explains. "I like that mentality of racing, where you just kind of go, go, go and are constantly trying to push the pace."

The move to Belgium was unprecedented. Page found himself in the position of being one of the only cyclists in the US that not only focused on cyclocross as his main sport, but even moved overseas to do it. "If you look at it in terms of what I've gotten out of the sport and things that I've accomplished so far, I'd say yes, it's been worth it," he says, and then laughs. "If you look at sponsorship and monetarily, no, I don't think it was the best plan."

Page isn't bitter about the lack of money in the sport though, and sees the fruits of his labor in other ways: "Last night, a guy came up to me after a race and said, 'I appreciate what you've done for the sport, and it's huge and I really like the dedication that you put into it.' And it's nice to hear that. I wouldn't change it."

"It's better than sitting behind a desk, I can tell you that."

6: JUNIORS IN US CYCLOCROSS

"When I first started to go to races, you could have one guy in a race. I get ecstatic about how big 'cross is becoming in general. And what I say all the time when I announce is that what the Belgians worry about when they come to America to race. I don't think they worry about our elite riders just yet. But they watch our cub juniors, and they're freaked out. When you see 40 12-year-old kids on 'cross bikes dismounting and remounting as well as they do, you should be very frightened." –Richard Fries

While the elite field is populated by plenty of 30+ year old men, they've got some stiff competition finishing up high school and their years in the junior rankings. And with USA Cycling fully on board to support and promote junior cyclocrossers in the US and in Europe, this burgeoning demographic might just be giving the top pros a run for their money in just a couple of years. Case in point is the U23 National Champion from 2012, Zach McDonald, who went on to place fourth in the Elite Championships less than 24 hours later. In New England, racers like Luke Keough are tearing it up and taking series titles, just years after being in the junior races.

However, there simply isn't as much money as there should be devoted to developing youth in the sport. But thanks to coaches like Geoff Proctor, at least steps are being taken in the right direction. He is quick to note that, "We don't have any junior development structure for cyclocross, and there's just so much more that we could be doing."

USA Cycling's Marc Gullickson is no stranger to cyclocross. A former National Champion, he understands more than most the importance of preparing juniors in the US to compete at the top levels. "We have grown the support for the junior program in the last few years," he says.

"We bring our top juniors over to Europe but it's tough in cyclocross because the season is during the school year and when you talk about juniors you have to talk about school."

What is our biggest strength in the US is also our downfall for creating the next World Champion though, and Gullickson is quick to add, "The strength of our US scene makes it tough to pull these kids away to get them to Europe, but there are a few times during the year, soft spots with few races, where we can get those kids to Europe." To that end, USA Cycling has gotten behind coach and mentor Geoff Proctor's EuroCrossCamp. Gullickson raves about the program, which shepherds great young US talent to Europe for the Christmas week of cyclocross (a time period of about 10 days with at least five races).

Why take juniors to Europe at Christmas? "We had our Nationals in early December and then there was this six week block of nothing," Proctor explains. "I went through that as a rider when I was racing Worlds, training by myself to prepare. It was obvious that there was a huge gap in our racing opportunities, so I wanted to start going to Belgium because there were a lot of races going on during that time."

Practicality came into play too: the juniors were in high school, and Under 23 racers were in college. So therefore, Proctor says, "I wanted to keep kids in school though, so I wanted to do it over Christmas vacation. Going to Europe at Christmas isn't easy for young guys, since it's such an important holiday at home in America, whereas in Belgium it's still cyclocross season and it's just different culturally. It's not easy and it's not for everybody."

"That timeframe he puts that on is a great timeframe for bringing our developing riders over to Europe," Gullickson says. "And we have a summer camp that Geoff runs in Montana where we try to pull our best young riders together to talk about training and what they need to do to succeed."

Proctor's logic for starting the camp was simple: "I'd done it the hard way, teaching myself to do cyclocross, so helping riders try to structure their season and helping them with opportunities was great. I started EuroCrossCamp in 2003 and was helping Bruce [Fina] get the USGP going. That all happened around the same time."

As a teacher himself, Proctor is skilled at dealing with junior and Under 23 racers as they come into their own as racers. "It's been a real challenge to balance my teaching with the coaching. It's too bad cyclocross isn't a summer sport. It's difficult to be away from school," he says. "But I enjoy helping young people, whether it's in the classroom or literally in the trenches at a 'cross race."

Even without USA Cycling and Geoff Proctor egging juniors along, the scene is developing fast and deep in the US. Oftentimes, juniors are topping the podiums in the Cat 3 Men's races, even though they would typically be ranked separately, and it is only UCI rules that prevent these young racers from jumping into the elite races before they hit 17.

But for Proctor, EuroCrossCamp is a junior's best hope for improving. "To race six times at Christmas, that's great experience you're gaining," he claims. "You can't just go to the World Championships anymore and expect to do anything if you don't have that investment."

Luke Keough

Watching top-level talent emerge in the Under 23 category and then translate into the pro field isn't unique to cyclocross, and Luke Keough's cycling abilities have the 20-year-old in high demand on both road and cyclocross bikes. But though he's only 20, Keough has 16 years of racing, and two racer older brothers ahead of him paving the way for what's bound to be a stellar career.

He's been on a bike since the tender age of five, though he approached cycling in a backwards fashion. "My oldest brother, Jake, saw one of my dad's friend's son race BMX one day and loved it. He wanted to do it.

So he got into BMX and we all followed in his footsteps. It's a family affair. My dad started riding a BMX bike to help me get over the jumps, so he could ride and push me over them because I was too small to get over them by myself. I started racing BMX when I was five years old."

© Pedal Power Photography

And once the family started, there was no stopping them and their upward, winning trajectory. "We're all on bikes. Jake transitioned over to 'cross and it's addicting. You get out there, ride around in the mud and have fun. It was an easy transition. The community was super cool."

So, as a 14-year-old junior racer, Luke started racing 'cross. Not necessarily for fun though: at first, it was to fix a problem the brothers were having in the BMX scene. "It was actually a transition to train for BMX, because one of our friends told us about it. We were always small on the BMX bikes, stature-wise, and big, overdeveloped 15-16 year olds were our biggest downfall. We were trying to look for an advantage, and a friend recommended trying 'cross. He said it would be a good way to build endurance. I started on a little mountain bike in the junior race, and it took off from there."

It didn't take long for Luke to start achieving results in the sport, and perhaps it was his BMX background that led to his notoriety as a sprinter. Results came quickly for the junior: "My first big result was the 15-16 National Championships in Providence, Rhode Island, which was basically a home race for my family and me, I had all my friends down there. I wasn't really expecting to win but I won by 40 seconds. I still remember that. It was one of my favorite results, my first national results."

And the list just keeps growing when it comes to his junior palmares. "After that, I had the 17-18 National Championships, won the USGP as a junior and as a U23. I have four wins at Cycle-Smart International, those wins are always big for me, I always like them."

But Keough's biggest result wasn't on American soil. Even as a junior just getting into the sport, he was heading across the pond to try his luck against the top riders in the world, and finding he could hang with the best of them. " I got fifth at a World Cup in Belgium as a junior and that sort of solidified the fact that I could compete at the World level. I was kind of up there, but that changed the mentality of everything."

Since then, he's most recently taken the win in the Shimano Pro Series in New England, not as a U23 racer, but in the elite men's field.

Logan Owen

To be described as the "Next Nys," after Sven Nys, the European "King of 'Cross," is a huge honor. To be described as the Next Nys on a cover of *Cyclocross Magazine* while still racing in the Junior 17-18 field ... that gives Americans hope for eventual dominance of European 'cross, and soon. Just wait until Logan Owen can race in UCI events.

While he's still not out of high school, Owen has been with Redline Bicycles for most of his life, starting from the time he was five years old, when he, like the Keoughs, was a BMX racer. His cyclocross career started with when he was testing their new Conquest 24 at age nine. The first time he used the bike was at Nationals in Portland, Oregon. He took second in that race, but by 2005 Nationals, he began his winning streak that would continue into 2011 when he took the 17-18 title. He says that title was his "toughest National Championship to win." This year, he says, "Everyone in the junior category was very close in skill last year, making it a tough race to overcome."

Owen might be young, but he's raced in Europe more than most elite racers in the US will ever get the chance to do. Having been there, he says that, "Racing in the U.S. is more relaxed and less technical. European racing has crazy steep drops and the riders race much more on the offensive rather than defensive." As a junior racer who's been groomed to race in Europe, he thinks that the future of the sport does, in fact, lie with the juniors coming up now. "I believe that the sport will grow immensely and more juniors will be involved with cycling. This will hopefully progress more US riders to the top of the sport to challenge the European competitors."

Despite his professional palmares at such a young age, he stays grounded, and firmly believes in keeping his options open. "My main goal for the future is becoming a professional cyclist but until that happens I plan on going to college and get my degree in pharmaceuticals."

This elite racer is also a high school student who counts his parents as his main support. He says, "My parents are very supportive of my racing and really help me get to all the races. Without their help I wouldn't be where I am today."

And how does Owen feel about being compared to Nys? Those are big (cycling) shoes to fill, but Owen isn't nervous about the comparison. "To be compared to Sven Nys is a huge honor being that he is such a great cyclist. I would love to achieve everything he has."

Zach McDonald

"I knew how good Jeremy was, and knew how good Zach was. I knew he'd have an impact on the Under 23 field, but didn't realize to what degree he'd actually take on all the seniors at the same time." Zach shocked not just his team manager, Slate Olson of Rapha-Focus, but the rest of the US as well when he placed fourth at Nationals in the elite men's race after winning the Under 23 race. Not only did he take fourth place, he took it after a crash in the first lap put him towards the back of the pack, and he flew like a bat out of hell, race face on, through the stung out line of racers searching for glory. When he caught up with the lead group, he didn't let up.

"I was 14 when I first got into it," McDonald explains. "I'd been doing a lot of mountain biking and road riding, and worked at a bike shop. They told me I should try cyclocross since I was doing the other two sports, and that I'd probably be good at it. So I said, 'OK, I'll try it,' and kept going from there."

It wasn't quite love at first race, but Geoff Proctor gave him the push that he needed by inviting McDonald to participate in the first incarnation of EuroCrossCamp. "He had a spot on the roster for EuroCrossCamp that first year, so I went over, and got pummeled in Europe. I decided I needed to be faster, and decided to train the next year and see what I could do."

With some stellar results, McDonald says that by January of that year, "I started talking with Slate [Olsen] a bit about the team, Rapha-Focus, and that was it."

McDonald started on Rapha-Focus the next year, much to his parent's delight. "They were glad when I found a team, that's for sure," he laughs. "They were my pit crew, essentially, so they were rather happy when I found a team and didn't have to have them be my 'sponsors.' Now they can come to races to watch and enjoy them!"

Since then, his star has been on the rise, and if you ask anyone who's been around the block, McDonald is the next greatest hope for US cyclocross. "If you go back to my junior years, my second year as a junior, I got some decent results in Europe and got on a couple of podiums over there," McDonald modestly admits. "Last year, 2011, was a good year, getting closer to the top ten in Europe, and winning U23 Nationals here, that was a highlight, as well as getting on the Elite Nationals podium."

As far as being the youngest on the team at only 21 years of age, McDonald doesn't feel like the little kid, by any means. "Chris Jones and I get along super well," he says. "We both have the same kind of relaxed attitude and just personalities that get along well. Powers came in and it didn't change anything. We get along great, we're all kind of on the same page, we all know what's going on. I'm the youngest but I've still been doing the Euro thing for five years now."

Even though cyclocross is closely associated with beer and partying, that isn't the case for the pros, who have training, flying and—in Zach's case—school to contend with. So, does this recently-legal racer have a normal college life? Doubtful.

"I wouldn't say I have a normal life during cyclocross season. Last season it was fly Friday, race Saturday and Sunday, fly home Monday and have class Monday through Thursday. Then do it again. But, at least with cyclocross you only have to train a couple hours a day during the season."

The juniors are surpassing the elites in some races: Luke Keough took control of the Shimano Pro Series and won the overall elite title at 20 years old.
© Pedal Power Photography

7: ELITE WOMEN IN US CYCLOCROSS

The elite women of cyclocross are an even more varied bunch than the top men in US 'cross. Because of the difficulties women in the sport still face when it comes to finding and securing sponsorships and salaries for racing, racers tend to not be focused solely on their two-wheeled career. Rather, a look at the top racers shows that even at the highest level, these women are still coaches, students, hairdressers, masseuses and any number of other careers on top of being racers. Additionally, because women mature differently than men on a biological level, and because women tend to come into the sport of cycling later than men do, thanks to a lack of support for junior girls, the age disparities on the podiums are even greater. Katie Compton and Kaitie Antonneau took first and second at elite women's Nationals in 2012. The two are separated by nearly fifteen years in age, and their racing histories couldn't be more dissimilar. By comparison, Ryan Trebon and Jeremy Powers, two constant rivals in the elite men's field, started racing at nearly the same time under similar circumstances and are separated by a mere two years.

However, the differences between the women of cyclocross seem only to strengthen bonds between them. In Compton and Antonneau's case, though the two are rivals, Compton serves as Antonneau's coach and mentor.

Additionally, the lack of sponsor interest in women has only served to make the women who have "made it" in the sport become more creative. Mo Bruno Roy has carved a niche for herself as one of the most sponsor-able athletes in the sport based on her stellar results, bubbly personality, and her ability to turn her personal choices, like a vegan diet, into something that lines sponsors like Bob's Red Mill, up at her door.

Katie F'n Compton

Katie Compton is perhaps the only racer from the US that's well-known worldwide, and for good reason. While she has yet to win at Worlds, she's come remarkably close year after year, and with Worlds coming to Louisville, smart money would be on Katie (after all, the Worlds site is near the Kentucky Derby, so what kind of race would it be without a little off-track betting?). With eight elite National Championship titles to her name, Compton is a safe bet.

© Dejan Smaic

However, Compton wasn't brought up on knobby tires and hurling herself over barriers. Rather, she was a road and track racer before hitting the dirt.

"I kind of stumbled into it because I was racing road and track when I was a junior, and got into racing mountain when I was a late junior, probably a senior in high school. I really liked mountain biking and had a couple of bad experiences on the road, so I decided I didn't want to do that anymore. I had just gotten back from Europe and it didn't go well, and I had taken a semester off of school, so I was kind of between semesters and had some free time."

It's a good thing for the sport that Compton's semester off found her hanging out with friends in a bar. "I used that free time to drink more than I probably should have and ride my bike as I felt like it. I was hanging out with friends in a bar, friends who had tried to talk me into cyclocross with how fun it is and how great it is, and I said, 'no way in hell,' and they said how good I'd be at it. I was like, 'I don't want to do it, it's stupid, I don't want to run, I want to ride my bike.' I think I had one more beer, enough to be like, 'Yeah, sure.' So I kind of got started by making decisions in a bar one night, thinking it was something that might be fun to do that I'd just gotten tired of saying no to."

And the aftermath? "I did a race in New Jersey, I got second. And I think I threw up afterwards. I raced it on my single speed mountain bike and loved it and had a great time. I think I was hooked every weekend after that."

That first race was in 1999, but Compton "didn't even think about going pro until 2005 or 2006." Of course, part of that could be the culture shift we've seen in cyclocross in the past few years: as it steadily grew in the US, the chances for Compton to pursue a legitimate career in the sport also grew.

As a cyclocross fan, you'll most likely hear people refer to Compton as KFC, or Katie F'n Compton (or the less child-appropriate Katie f***ing Compton). It's a term of endearment in the scene, and the best way to explain it is to hear about its origin: "It was the season I was winning a lot of races and I think it was one of my best seasons. A friend of a friend asked about who won the 'cross race, and the response was, 'Katie F--in Compton, who else would win the 'cross race?' It was thrown out like a joke that way but it kind of took off. Then my friend started calling me KFC and made a t-shirt for me after 2007 Worlds when I got the silver medal and it just caught on after that."

Compton hasn't always been confident in herself, and for her, one of the best moments she's had in cyclocross came when she unexpectedly won her first National Championship, in 2004. "It was amazing because I had no idea I could do it. I had been racing well in Colorado, no one really knew who I was. I started at the back of the group and raced all the way through the group. It was a muddy, hard day. I just had a really good day and surprised myself that I won and that felt really great. I remember the night before the race, Mark and I were sleeping on a futon in my friend's basement in Portland and we were like, 'how cool would it be if I won tomorrow?' and thinking how exciting that would be. It was a long shot, one of those 'what if?' conversations. And so I thought about that after winning that race, and the 'what if?' turned into reality.

COMPTON'S BEST WORST DAY

"It was the World Cup at Roubaix. That was really awesome to win, especially since it was just a tough race to win. I think I've won there twice. But one was really important because there was a false start, and I realized that if there's a false start, you should just go, instead of waiting for the gun, because if you don't, everyone else will just pass you. So I learned that the hard way. I hesitated and everyone swarmed and I got off the velodrome in last place, and it just pissed me off. I was like, 'Are you kidding me?' And so I ended up chasing the whole field and racing angry and pissed off but it worked out really well. I think it took two laps to get to the front, and I got to the front and I just attacked and went for it again and got a gap. It was a technical muddy day and it was fun and I felt good. And then on top of having that kind of start, it felt really good to win."
                                                                    –Katie Compton

Kaitlin Antonneau

Kaitie Antonneau is of the next generation of elite cyclocrossers, but unlike U23 men like McDonald, she's already racing with the elite women, since there isn't a U23 Women's category (or a junior women's category at Worlds). Kaitie is already in a league of her own, at 19 years old. With a tenth place at a World Cup and a second place overall at US Elite Women's Nationals, she's on her way to becoming the "next Katie Compton," which works out well, since that's been her goal all along.

"I want to follow in Katie's footsteps. She leads by a very excellent example. I want to be that accomplished like her when I get older. She coaches me and I always watch her, I watch her pre-ride sometimes, I watch videos of her on youtube for some races, when I was younger I'd watch videos of her racing. Even though she didn't do as well at Worlds as she wanted to, she's still one of the best in the world."

Of course, even though Antonneau is only 19, she's not exactly a "newbie" on the bike. "We live ten minutes from the velodrome at home (in Wisconsin) and my mom took me and my sister down there one summer, so that summer, they had stock races and I just raced every Monday on my bike from Walmart. The next summer, my mom got my sister and me BMX bikes, it was kind of serious and really competitive but it was fun. When I was old enough—when I was ten—to go on the actual track, I started doing that. And I just fell in love with it, I guess. I've been doing it for a while."

And then came cyclocross. "When I was 12, I did my first cyclocross race on a mountain bike, just a local race. And I don't know, I did Nationals on it the next year and I won, and I was like, 'this is cool, I like winning,' so then I just kept doing it. I think it's just a thing, over time, it's a thing I found I wanted to do more of it all the time. I'm drawn to it. I don't know if that makes sense but it's my favorite out of all of the disciplines."

While Antonneau may look up to Compton, there's another layer to their relationship, other than simply friendly competitors: Compton is Antonneau's coach and mentor. "I started coaching her a couple of years ago. She started showing promise on the cross bike and she was naturally good at it. She's a good racer, she knows how to suffer. She's been super fun to coach. She's such a smart, fun, talented girl and it's been fun to see her progression. I don't ever have to repeat myself. I don't know how she does it. She's quick on the uptake, it makes my job really easy."

And while Antonneau's favorite moment was crossing the Nationals finish line and going to hug Compton, Compton's take on that moment was equally emotional: "That was actually one of my favorites too. I think I got more satisfaction watching her cross the line than when I did. She was just so excited when she won. It couldn't have been a better Nationals for her. I was almost in tears."

So where is Antonneau headed? The safe bet is that in coming years, we'll see the two "Katies" locking horns (or handlebars) more frequently in races as Antonneau comes into her own as a racer. But that said, she's aware that cyclocross may never pay the bills, so when I asked what she wanted to do when "she grows up," she answered: "Race my bike? Yeah. When I'm done here with school, I'd like to race my bike as long as I can, and if it doesn't work out, that's why I'm in school."

Nicole Duke

© Dejan Smaic

Unlike Antonneau, who is at the very beginning of her career, Nicole Duke has been racing for years, and while Antonneau's non-race weekends are spent catching up on homework and studying, Duke is a mom of two and has a hair-dressing business on the side. But despite her lack of time to focus solely on a career on the bike, Duke has made her way to the top of the pro women's field in the US, pulling in a third place at Nationals in 2011 and taking the second-best American results in Elite Women's Worlds.

How does a mom manage to get herself into cyclocross? Oddly enough, cyclocross is a less extreme version of the sport she loves. "It started when I was a downhiller. We had a team here and in Boulder we have Wednesday Worlds, a practice race session. Years ago, in the late 90s, I'd done that a few times and that's when I first heard about 'cross and realized what it was, but I never raced."

After hearing about 'cross for years, Nicole finally went for it. "I started doing short track MTB events for fun because they were short and sweet, so I didn't have to make much of a commitment. It was the end of the short track season and the next race at this place was a cyclocross race. I did it on my MTB and got third and I realized, 'This is perfect for me.' It's short, sweet and technical. I got to hang out with the girls. I guess that was 2007, and I've been doing it ever since."

Like most of the pros who started racing "just for fun," or "just as a workout," Duke says, "I started to fall in love with the sport so much that I just kind of got sucked in by the culture."

And that led to racing. "In 2007 I raced casually, then took 2008 off because I was pregnant. I didn't even know if I'd get back into it. Then in 2009, I got a bike and got into it casually again, and did well locally. Then I asked Subaru if I could race for them, and what that did was give me more motivation because I had pressure because I was racing for myself and for a team, so there were expectations. I started training and thinking and preparing for it more. That was when I started to get more serious, in 2010."

Duke's seriousness paid off and the results came fast. "I was pleasantly surprised by my results. I hadn't trained as much as everyone else but being older and knowing my body and knowing how to train and being efficient with all of that stuff just paid off. I went to my first USGP at the Derby Cup and no one knew who I was and I got seventh both days. Then I realized I could do this at a higher level, and I hadn't realized my body could do that."

That result paled in comparison to what the next year would bring, and in 2010, Duke got her first Masters National Championship jersey.

One of her favorite moments wasn't a major win, but rather, getting past a mechanical hurdle that almost ruined a run for second in the USGP series in 2011. "For me, the Bend USGP sticks out. I was close to being second but had that mechanical and it was gut-wrenching, to have a great race and lose it there. But I got up and ran as hard as I could, I was killing myself, and I didn't know it at the time, but that put me in second overall in the USGP series. To be second overall in the series in my second pro year of racing was a huge accomplishment and really unexpected. I hadn't even looked at the points, really."

Despite her accomplishments, Duke remains humble, saying, "At this point in my career, being older and having kids, I'm just taking what I can get." Luckily, she can get a lot.

Laura Van Gilder

When you watch Laura Van Gilder race, it seems like cyclocross was what she was born to do. But despite her 23 years of racing, it wasn't until recently she picked up a 'cross bike, just to keep herself busy in her off-season. As a road racer and USA Crit champion, Van Gilder's sprint is legendary. And it turns out it translated very well to cyclocross.

"It was four years ago, after 2008. I decided I'd really like a motivating goal to keep me going. I typically ride straight through the fall and winter but I found that I wanted something to do. A friend and my boyfriend had always mentioned cyclocross and I had always thought, 'I'm too tired from the road.' I decided I was ready to give it a shot and I loved it immediately for a lot of reasons."

© Pedal Power Photography

For Van Gilder, she didn't like it because it came naturally, rather, she says, "I liked how engaging the sport was, it was testing you on so many different levels: athletically, technically, and mentally. I liked that you had many opportunities throughout the course of the race to improve. If you make a mistake on a part of the course, you have a chance to come around it again three or four times to do it better. I felt like there were constant rewards and challenges on a course." Surprisingly, she prefers the break from her career as a sprinter, saying, "I liked that it took the emphasis off the final sprint at the end of the race."

As a former mountain biker, Van Gilder found that cyclocross "embodied some of the things I really like about racing." Because a career on the road prevents Van Gilder from being able to mountain bike during the summer months, 'cross is a great way for her to utilize the technical skills that she had honed in her early days of racing, 23 years ago.

"Living on the East Coast and having such a different variety of races to choose from on any given weekend, my first year I raced 70 races on the road, upgraded to Cat 2 and realized I had a natural ability. My boyfriend had prepared me for the challenges from road racing, and I learned a lot in a short amount of time and had a lot of success. I loved it from the beginning."

But even with her impressive set of palmares on the road, Van Gilder never dreamed a career in cyclocross would be a reality. When asked, she laughs and says, "Absolutely not. Number one, I didn't know what I was getting into really. I'd read about it, but I had no idea. Especially because I'd been out of mountain biking for so long, I didn't know what my technical skills were going to be like. I think I came in when it started getting bigger and more mainstream. Now, so many roadies are coming over, and it's gotten so much more competitive. It was so exciting, and I continued to learn."

The lack of pressure on her to perform at the level she'd been racing on the road made her first year in cyclocross magical. "That first year was great. I'm still on the same team, C3, and that was huge. It was a welcome change. Yes, you're competing against the people, but you're also trading insight on the course. We were tooth and nail out there on the course, yet we often talk about the course and how to dial it in. And that was amazing. That first season as a whole, I'm just really starry-eyed about it."

But when you ask Van Gilder to remember some of her best results on the 'cross bike, she says, "I can only think back to the epicness of races. Granogue in the mud, and Beacon in the hurricane. I think back about times that I've suffered through, or were hard fought. Maybe they weren't victories but they were hard fought races. The races themselves, they overlap."

Of course, she's being more modest than anything, with plenty of wins under her belt, including the most recent, the overall victory in the Shimano New England Pro Cyclocross Series, as well as countless UCI wins on the East Coast in the past few years.

In fact, her early wins actually make racing now even harder: "Since that first season, I've felt more pressure, and because of that, more disappointment. It's hard to live up to that, and the field is more competitive now. People are coming in who have better engines and better technical skills."

Though she now has more competition with young talent like Kaitie Antonneau coming up into the elite field, she still loves the sport and has no plans to leave it. She gets nostalgic for those early days just a few years back though, and says, "We should nurture everything about it, especially the atmosphere that all of us remember. Remember those aspects of it, because that's what's going to keep feeding it." And while embracing the grassroots beginnings that the US is so proud of, she adds, "Then you can embrace the professional end, so you can have sponsored riders competitive at a world level, and world class events here. Hopefully it won't flame out."

Amy Dombroski

Amy Dombroski might be young—she's only 25—but she's one of the few racers in the US brave (or arguably, crazy) enough to spend most of her season living and racing in Europe. But even though she has dedicated so much of her time to the sport of cycling, it wasn't her first love. In fact, she says, "I started in 2006 and I had moved to Colorado to pursue ski racing."

But the career in ski racing simply wasn't meant to be. "I had a knee injury there, which brought me to Boulder to do rehab. My brother told me to jump on a bike for rehab so I did that and the competition bug started eating at me. I jumped in a road race and fell in love with cycling really quickly."

© Pedal Power Photography

Road racing just whet Dombroski's appetite for more cycling, and she says, "Once that season was over, I knew I wasn't ready to stop." So again, her brother came to the rescue and the two got a cyclocross bike together and went to a local park. But it wasn't love at first sight for her. "My brother showed me how to do the dismounts and I remember hating it. I was in tears because I couldn't get it. But something about it …"

She wanted to quit, but says, "I felt guilty because he'd gotten me the bike, so I kept trying." And it paid off, because Dombroski laughs and explains, "Then, that year I won the Under 23 National Championships and I thought, 'OK, something is clicking.'"

And like so many of the other elite racers have said, "I fell in love with cyclocross. I like cycling but cyclocross is the one that grabbed me."

Maybe it was the winning streak Dombroski was on. "I was OK at ski racing," she says, "But I didn't win many races. So to get that win at Nationals, I realized, 'Oh, I could be good at something!' And it was the first time my dad came to a cyclocross race. It was a breakthrough for me, thinking, 'I can actually do something with this sport.'"

But the sport in the US wasn't enough for Dombroski. "I was racing professionally on the road with WebCore and we went to Europe to race and I loved it there. The competition is just that much harder, so with an underlying love of cyclocross, I wanted to go see the motherland of cyclocross, Belgium, and try it out."

As a 21-year-old falling in love with the sport, Dombroski made her move in 2008 and headed to Europe for her first World Championship, following the World Cup at Hoogerheide. "It really grabbed me. It was a combination of just being in Europe and then the crowds. You feel like a rock star when you're over there, as opposed to here, where it's your dad cheering you on and that's about it. Over there, it's an event."

Dombroski still loves the racing in the US, make no mistake. "The racing in the US is so good," she clarifies. "By racing in Belgium, I'm by no means putting the racing in the US down. And of course, I love coming back to the US and when other people come over to race in Europe."

That said, her best and favorite results do come from the big European races. She says, "The one I'm most proud of is getting sixth this year at the Plzen World Cup because I think it was just a huge breakthrough race for me. Not a lot of Americans have finished that far up, so I think that kind of showed my potential. That's why I'm excited about going back."

Mo Bruno Roy

Like Dombroski, native New Englander Mo Bruno Roy spends a good chunk of her time racing in Europe, though in recent years she's made the shift to a more domestically oriented schedule. And why not, with the advent of the Shimano Pro Series practically in her backyard, and the USGP series sharing a major sponsor in Bob's Red Mill. At first glance, Bruno Roy is a bubbly, friendly, and most importantly, fast and strong cyclocross racer. And when you take another look, it's easy to spot just how business-savvy she is as well.

© Pedal Power Photography

Obtaining and keeping sponsors is key in any sport at the elite level, but in cycling in general and cyclocross in particular, for women, it's often hard to come by. Often, elite women racers—no matter how good their results—are forking over credit cards and racking up debt to pay to race for, generally speaking, less payout than the men. Bruno Roy, like Adam Myerson or Molly Cameron, has managed to successfully market herself—an elite cyclocrosser with a passion for vegan cooking and massage—to become one of the most well-known and well-liked female racers in the country. In an industry that tends to overlook women, she's made quite a name for herself.

"I got into cyclocross via being a soigneur for pro teams and getting more exposure to cycling that way," she explains. "But before that, I was exposed to cycling through mountain biking through Tim Johnson, who went to high school with me. He raced 'cross, and so did a group of friends from the North Shore [in Boston] when it was super grassroots in 1995. I was able to go to a few and try out a bike. I thought it was fun but didn't get back into it until 2004."

However, in 2004, she hit the ground running. "I was part of a local women's team sponsored by a local clog shop," she laughs. "I was able to join them and try cyclocross, and I bought my own bike and gave it a go. I did well enough in that season that I was encouraged to go to Nationals and try racing bigger races."

It snowballed from there, and by her second season, she was racing for Stu Thorne's CyclocrossWorld team, and they were able to give her a second bike ("on loan," she's quick to add). "And I progressed from there," she says. Then, the next year, she took off. "I got third at Elite Nationals and won Masters Nationals in Providence in the snowstorm and that was the launching point for everything."

"I thought I was just doing it for fun," she adds, "But that was sort of a turning point for me. My results had gotten me way farther than I ever thought I'd get. I didn't have aspirations to do that, I thought it was for fun. It's been great, and it's also been really challenging to keep up that level when I stumbled upon it, in a way."

Enter the sponsors. Today, Bruno Roy stands out in a race in her all-white Bob's Red Mill skinsuit, and she's incredibly proud of the life she's built for herself as a racer. Before Bob's came into the picture, she'd ridden for CyclocrossWorld, and from there, she'd gone on to Independent Fabrication. After that, she developed a bike sponsorship with Seven Cycles, and relationships with companies including SRAM and Mavic. Still, like most elite racers just starting out, cash sponsors were harder to come by. "I had my bikes, but no financial support for racing," she says, "So Matt [her husband] and I started our own team, MM Racing, and made our own kits and paid for all of that ourselves and I kept working full time."

Then, in 2010, Bruno Roy did something different. "I wrote to Bob's Red Mill, because they sponsored the USGP series and I loved the product. I figured it was worth writing to them and seeing if they were sponsoring any individual athletes."

It wasn't an overnight fairytale ending, and, "They wrote back that they didn't have a marketing budget that extended to any kind of cycling sponsorship but they could send me as much as oatmeal and grains as I wanted. I got so much oatmeal, which I couldn't have been happier about." She laughs as she describes the boxes and boxes of oats that appeared at their door.

However, the following season, Bob's Red Mill contacted Bruno Roy and said that they were interested in sponsoring an athlete. Now, they're her primary sponsor and it has allowed her to change how she races. "That's taken a huge load off because it's allowed me to cut back my work schedule. I'm still not making any money doing this sport but I'm not paying off an extensive credit card bill."

Bruno Roy is a sponsor's dream come true because even after securing the sponsorship, she's continued to work to promote the brand in ways other than just emblazoning their name on her kit. "We decided to send out a newsletter and signed onto Twitter and Facebook to promote the things that we did. We continued on that trend with Bob's Red Mill and Seven Cycles in order to really give back," she explains. "If sponsors don't see a return on investment, they aren't going to be interested in continuing sponsorship beyond a season, if that, or stepping forward again. Especially for a company not in the cycling industry."

Even though, since getting sponsors and gaining popularity, Bruno Roy has been able to spend time racing all over the country and the world, her best season, in her account, was the first season she did. "It was at one of the last races I did that season," she recalls. "It was one of the best races I did in terms of having the ability to see that I had some potential in the sport. I came from running and I always felt really clumsy attached to a machine. It was snowy and icy and I saw that there was an element of running and riding in that race, and it was the more technical style of riding the bike. I'd say that was my favorite. Being able to see the potential."

For Bruno Roy, who started as a runner before she took to the knobby tires, when asked about her favorite moment in cyclocross, she waxes poetic. "Anytime I can get off my bike and run as fast as I can and feel really strong doing it. Getting on and off the bike and there's an effortlessness and a gracefulness to it. Those are my favorite parts of cyclocross."

8: LOOKING FOR EQUALITY—HOW CYCLOCROSS IS CHANGING WOMEN'S CYCLING

"If you look at the performance of US racers at Worlds in the past five years, our women are getting on the podium."

–Joan Hanscom

Women race just as hard as the men but struggle for equality in cycling.
© Pedal Power Photography

How has cyclocross changed for women over the years? "Well, first of all, there are women's fields," Mark Vareschi laughs. "When I started racing in New York, there were one or two women and no women's field. Then, when I started racing in New England, there were 15 to 20 women in one field. And now we're getting 40 or more in each of the two women's fields. I think some of the fastest growth we've seen has been in women's cyclocross."

When you talk about women in cycling, gender issues of equal payouts, equal sponsorships, difficulties in women's equipment, and lack of respect for women as professional cyclists inevitably have to be included in the discussion. Cyclocross has proven to be one of the most equality-driven forms of competitive cycling, with many US races offering equal payouts and races immediately before the elite men's race, rules that require any UCI C1 race to have a women's field, and the big name teams like Rapha-Focus, Cannondale-CyclocrossWorld.com and Raleigh all working to add more women to their rosters. Additionally, since cyclocross grew organically and with such small women's fields until only recent years, the friendships and bonds formed between the elite women, regardless of team loyalties, have led to a more welcoming scene for women at all levels. The approachability of the elite racers has also allowed the sport to grow more for amateur women than it has in other disciplines.

© Pedal Power Photography

In fact, elite racer Mary McConneloug thinks that this growth is simply attributable to the nature of 'cross. "I feel like this sport can appeal to those tough individuals who like to work hard and push personal limits," she says, adding, "It's also a great feeling to get super fit, improve skills, and meet other cool people … It is not just a man's sport. There are so many incredibly talented athletic women and the stereotype of hard women racing bikes is changing—we can be soft, beautiful and charge on the bike." She laughs and adds, "Plus, we're probably much more fun to watch racing than men."

Cyclocross might be bigger in Europe than it is in the US, but for the women, there's no place like home. This is a great time for women in the sport, and a great time for women to get involved in the sport. Duke says, "I'm really impressed with women's cyclocross in the US, as far as media attention, personalities, respect levels. I think cyclocross is doing a lot for women's cycling at this point. In Europe, the sport is more popular but I feel like women in the States get more respect and I think it's just a difference between personalities in the different countries. It's a really exciting time to be a woman in cyclocross in the US and there's a lot of movement happening. It's nice to be a part of it."

It has come a long way, and even in New England, one of the first places where racing was popular, women's cycling wasn't a big priority. Mo Bruno Roy recalls, "In my first race, there was a women's category—women's open—and there were 10 to 15 women, so now to see a Cat 3/4 field with over 100 riders is a phenomenal difference in a short amount of time."

To that end, while there are problems within women's cycling, the overall growth is positive. Bruno Roy adds, "The participation, especially in women's racing, is really encouraging more and more people to try it out. Cyclocross is pretty welcoming. There's a social aspect to it, a duration aspect to it which is manageable, and I think it's a lot less scary than road or mountain bike racing if you're just getting into it."

With women's cycling seeing such huge growth in the US and in Europe, it's interesting to watch as the two continents struggle to make sense of women's racing. While Europe may have deeper fields for the pro women, and arguably better opportunities for women at the very top to land on good teams (Compton herself is on a Euro team now, Rabobank), the US has something that Europe hasn't gotten to yet: often, races have equal prize money for men and women, and at nearly every race, elite men and elite women race back-to-back. In Europe, women's races tend to be shunted to wee hours of the morning, leaving spectators underwhelmed.

In fact, Marc Gullickson is quick to note that for women, "It's tough because there's no World Championships for junior or U23 women." He suggests that the problem lies in the European model of cyclocross, which is outdated and tends toward a sexist slant emphasizing men's cycling. "The UCI cyclocross commission makes a lot of those rules, and it's tough because it's sort of an old boy's club, it's pretty much dictated by the heart of Belgian 'cross."

For Gullickson though, that just leaves more opportunity to work on women's racing in the US, and he believes that "we have better women racing in the States than they do over there."

If cyclocross is such a welcoming sport, then why are more women racing in the US than in Europe? The question goes back to the participant versus spectator nature of the sport, but also the level of difficulty on the courses. In Europe, usually only twenty or thirty women take to the start line, nearly half of the total of racers in the men's field. Antonneau suggests that "maybe it's because the courses over here are more geared towards B women—it's still really challenging, but in their own different way. It's welcoming to people, to lower categories. It's not as intense, you can do it for fun."

Geoff Proctor agrees, and would love to see more women racers from the US make their way to Europe. "The first EuroCrossCamp, I did bring two women, including Gina Hall, who won a race," he says. "It was one of the first US female wins in 'cross in Europe. But as it takes on a more developmental role, it's really hard because there aren't that many women's races until the past year, and it wasn't a great place for younger women to learn because the level was so high." He doesn't mean that the young women in Europe are faster, he's simply referring to the fact that Junior/Under-23 women still race with the elite women.

He adds, "I continue to think our women are so good here. The energy at the start of a women's race is easily equal to the men's."

As one of the longest-competing women in cyclocross, Compton has watched the growth of the sport for women in recent years. "I love seeing so many women on the start line. Nationals in Bend [two years ago] was the highest we've ever gotten. It's huge and I like to see that. It's crazy. I think we're going to get stronger and stronger and better and better women. It's got to be that natural progression, we've got stronger elite women, there are plenty of younger women coming up, so there's definitely going to be some good competition and racing in the long term."

However, the early days of close friendships among the elite athletes are in danger of being forgotten, says Laura Van Gilder. "I appreciated that camaraderie and yet, competitiveness. That's changed since I got into the sport, and I imagine it's because people are vying for the Worlds team and big sponsorship. It was more accessible when I began and I miss that. Everyone wants to win and do their best, but I'm sad to see that part of the sport go. It's a hard sport and we give up a lot to do it, so there should be fun times associated with it. We won't all make those big bucks."

And while the US women's fields may not be quite as deep as the men's fields just yet, they are coming out in record numbers, and race promoters are starting to question whether two women's fields (an elite field and an amateur field) are enough.

"When I was a downhiller and first heard about it, it was such a fringe sport and of course, it still is, but it seemed like only a few people were doing it. And just in the time I've been doing it, in four years time, racer participation has doubled, and it's the new exciting sport in cycling. It's dynamic, spectator-friendly and it's kind of a circus," Nicole Duke says. "There's such a great culture around it and I think people are really catching on. It seems like there's been a huge amount of growth. I don't think we've even begun to peak, so I'm very thankful to be in the sport at this moment in time. I'm thinking, is this just because I'm in it and around it all the time? But I talk to other people and people in the industry are like, 'no, this is big.'"

© Pedal Power Photography

That rapid growth that we've seen among the women should be embraced and promoted, and now is the time to do it. Mary McConneloug adds, "Let's keep it rolling! We need to continue to support women's racing and aim to reach the females out there that might be interested and get them involved. This sport has taught me so much, I feel many would like it and benefit from it, if they gave it a shot."

For women, while the sport is growing in leaps and bounds, there is one big problem facing promoters who have only a certain number of hours of daylight to conduct races. So then, the big problem becomes that of junior development. For the boys and men, there are 15-16, 17-18 and Under 23 fields either as standalone races or mixed into most larger races. For the women, the categories are simply elite and amateur. Because of this, and because of cyclocross's rapid growth, there are young women forced to either wait in the amateur field until they can race UCI races (there's an age limit), or they do race in the UCI races and are in over their heads.

However, when will women's racing reach that critical mass to the point that it focuses on junior development?

Antonneau, who did come into cyclocross as a junior, says, "I think it's more important to have a separate junior women 17-18 category for a world championship or something like that than it is for a separate U23 race. Having the 17-18 category at a World level I think will help the development of the sport for women. I think it's good for the U23 women to race with the 'big girls' because it helps us to push ourselves, makes us better, and then the jump isn't as big when you graduate from U23."

Paul Curley has been in 'cross long enough to have watched women come and go from the scene, sometimes because there wasn't anywhere for them to go. For him, young women are a big part of his ideal version of the future: "What I've advocated for with having Worlds in America for the first time is the inclusion of a junior women's race. I think that this would be the opportunity to get that. Europe has always focused on the elite cyclocross, they haven't had the masses and masses of people participating. They were watching it and drinking, but they weren't racing their bikes."

Of course, a focus on racer's development in Europe, regardless of age, might be the key to building a world-class group of elite women's racers in the US. Racers like Antonneau, Compton, Bruno Roy, Duke and Dombroski occasionally jaunt to Europe, but more often, the money simply isn't there, especially for women just starting to come up in the cyclocross world. For Compton, this is one of the biggest problems with cyclocross for women in the US. "I think our US women would do better with more experience and more consistent experience over in Europe. It makes it hard for them to show the world what they can actually do. I think we would if there was more money involved, if the women could afford to go over and do it. It's a huge investment."

Europe is beginning to make strides in terms of gender equality as compared to the US, though they have a long way to go. Promoter Brook Watts says, "I see Europe at a tipping point about how women's racing is being treated. We're now seeing at every C1 race worldwide, they have to offer a women's race. It seems like a small step, but it's a monster step for old school European race directors to embrace, and we're seeing a move towards a more even prize list."

It isn't a quick process though, and he adds, "We're seeing it done incrementally. I see it heading that way. While there's still some great inequities, like how women race at GvA [a Euro race] at 10 AM and there's a huge gap before the men go, but I think we're seeing that change. I think we'll start to see a greater appreciation of women's racing. We're certainly in the forefront here."

On the more amateur side of things, since most women just starting out aren't interested (yet) in racing in Europe, Compton has some key advice: "Just ask questions, it's not a big deal. That's what questions are for, and the cross world is pretty accommodating and people will try to help you out. It's an encouraging sport, it's inclusive, we're all out there kind of with the challenge against ourselves and the course."

The sport will continue to grow for the 'fairer sex,' but as Nicole Duke says, "Inevitably it will happen because it's already becoming more popular. But I think it's our job as elite riders and women in the sport to try to facilitate growth in the sport for other women."

And with this growth in the beginner field, the elite field will improve as well, and Joan Hanscom believes that, "The more women who race, the better the chances of finding that needle in the haystack, the next Kaitie Antonneau or Katie Compton."

How can the elite women be put into service? "I think there are already a lot of great women trying to do that, holding clinics and serving as role models for younger women. It's about introducing someone to it and giving them the tools and confidence and ability," Duke claims, "With the popularity and a lot more of these local races and it being a family event, a lot more women are getting curious about it. And I think it takes a woman leader out there saying, 'You can do this,' and getting women out there. The women of cyclocross are already doing that. It seems to be a more laid back culture, and since the races are so short and women are out there anyway, I think it's going to naturally happen."

Amy Dombroski also agrees about the clinic concept. "I think we should continue with development, and I think we're on the right way forward. I think we need to be patient though," she cautions. "It's not going to go from five participants to 500 participants overnight. I think in the US we've got all these clinics and that's a huge part of it. I've taught a bunch of women and kid specific clinics and I think the women's ones really help. To have an environment where they know they're not going to be with the men, it encourages women."

Promoters recognize the need for more women-oriented events as well, especially female promoters like Dorothy Wong and Joan Hanscom. "I'm planning on incorporating more women's events," Wong intonates, "and supporting women's cycling at all levels. I think we have to step up to represent and promote women and take that extra step."

And Wong doesn't believe that promoting women begins and ends with the elite field. "We need to market women as a complete package, she says, adding, "Nothing makes me happier than seeing these young kids racing bicycles. And then I see older women watching and saying, 'I wish I had started when I was your age.' I hear that so much. But then I'm like, 'You're out there! You're doing it at your age!'"

Companies are beginning to understand that supporting women is a win-win for them as well. As I interviewed various team managers and key people at cyclocross-oriented companies, most of them were quick to tell me that they had big plans for the women's division, from starting to build more high-level women specific 'cross bikes to adding more pro women to their teams to pushing for more clinics for beginner women. Slate Olson of Rapha emphasizes the point, saying, "We want to, as a team, show our investment in growing the sport for women." However, he does add that it's not always so simple to add to a team that's already in a good spot, no matter how beneficial it might be: "There's always a desire for me: 'We gotta do more, we gotta do bigger!' But sometimes you have to just keep your head down and do what you do well instead of worrying about accelerating or complicating."

Ladies: just as badass as the men, maybe even more. © Pedal Power Photography

EQUAL PAY FOR EQUAL WORK?

"I think it's growing. I think every promoter in the US is being challenged to have equal payout."   —Amy Dombroski

Promoters struggle with the question of equal pay for male and female racers. In Europe, almost without question, women don't make as much as the men in prize money. The US has always led the charge in that respect, but at quite a few races across the country, the gender divide still exists.

For this reason, elite racers like Laura Van Gilder believe that women are essentially forced to walk away from the sport eventually. "It's disappointing to go duke it out with the best riders in the country and walk away with $44 for a fifth place, considering what your equipment cost, or even just the cost of keeping it running. And a lot of us aren't getting that stuff for free. So at the end of the day, people are making choices. Women have a lot more on their plate, you're looking at probably an older age profile for most women, and maybe they're looking at it and realizing they're not getting much on their return."

Promoter Murphy Mack is pro-equal pay, and his logic is simple. "I always have equal payouts for men and women. The women must go the same distance and elevation, etc. that the men do. Equal pay for equal work right? If you're against that maybe you should come into the present century with the rest of us. Beyond that, I see offering equal payouts as a way to get all the women to the race. I guess you could say my equal payout brings all the girls to the yard."

Promoter Dorothy Wong agrees, saying, "Everyone can say they want equal pay and so do I. Any way we can showcase women, I will. Cyclocross is a great sport for all ages and sizes of women, especially if we can market it, and I feel so strongly about it."

She does, however, admit that there are problems with the concept of equal pay, when field sizes are vastly different and the spectators line up primarily to watch the men. "The challenge for women in sports is that we need an audience. Not that women aren't fun to watch but it's exciting when you see 100 guys charging out, and less so when there are only 20 women," and that, she believes, is where the problem comes in. "Paying 20 deep to women in the race is not helpful, from a promoter's standpoint."

That said, Wong is passionate that the women at the top deserve the same as the men at the top of the sport. "I strongly believe the top women should be paid the same as the top men. I've thought about putting on just a UCI race for women, instead of for men. I think there's huge potential we're not touching by not promoting the women enough."

However, other promoters disagree. Not because they hate women's racing, but for practical reasons.

Talking to Adam Myerson, a long time proponent of women's cycling, raises the two key arguments when it comes to paying women equally in the sport. He claims that the two ways to look at payouts are as pay for entertainment, or pay for work. And depending on how a promoter looks at the situation, the argument can be made in both directions.

"The first," he says, "is to look at it as entertainment, and entertainers get paid based on the value of the entertainment they return. And it doesn't matter if you're male or female, star power pulls in a certain amount of return. So if you're an actor or actress in Hollywood, what you bring in at the box office determines your pay scale. And I'm sure there's sexism in Hollywood, but it's not equal pay for equal work, it's equal pay for equal value of the work."

This applies to cyclocross, because, as he explains, "Sports are, in part, entertainment. So if men's racing is more popular, has more spectators, brings in more sponsors, then of course the athletes would get paid more money because they create more money, because it's more valued. Now I can say that I don't think that's OK, but it is what it is. So in that sense, as it stands, women shouldn't be paid as much as men."

However, Myerson doesn't believe that this is the final word on the issue. "I can say that I want to change that, I would like to affect change in that area and make it so women's cycling is as interesting, is as valued, as men's cycling. But what has to happen first?" he asks. "Do we start by giving them more prize money so more show up? So we get more entry fee money? We know that doesn't work. You can't throw money at the problem. You put up equal prize money for the women, they won't always come."

Promoters in recent years have tried this approach in all disciplines of cycling, with mixed results from race to race. "So many promoters who care, who've tried to do something like that and have gotten burned. Because it turns out, the women, while they want equal pay in the symbolic sense of it, really race because they love it," Myerson says. "And the money doesn't get them to show up. Even though they want it in principle, we've seen that equal prize money is not enough to get women to come."

If equal prize money won't get women to show up at the starting line, and women don't have the same 'entertainment value' as the men, it seems like the answer is that women's payouts don't need to equal those of the men. However, that's where Myerson's second point comes in: cycling is a job. "The other way to look at it is as a job," he says. "And if it's a job, then there absolutely has to be equal pay for equal work and it's absolutely unacceptable that women don't get paid equal prize money. Because it's a job and equal pay for equal work applies."

At the end of the day, cyclocross has the chance to be the first cycling discipline where men and women are treated equally, and Myerson believes that to be true, saying, "'Cross has an opportunity to show real equality."

Even women promoters agree that it's a tough situation. Joan Hanscom of the USGP Series says, "It's tricky. It's hard. We want to do the right thing. Women have to fly and pay for travel to races, and they don't get a discount on flights or hotels just because they're women and their race is 20 minutes shorter. So we think it's really important to pay them the same. They're racing just as hard."

She adds, "To build a professional class of athletes, you have to pay them professional prize money and I think giving Katie Compton $200 when the male winner is getting $2000, or whatever that discrepancy is, is a shame. We're fortunate that Exergy is insistent on prize equality. We were already leaning that way when they came on board, but Exergy allowed us to take the prize list all the way, 15 racers deep."

Team leader Stu Thorne thinks that the future can be bright for women in cyclocross, if the sport can grow, and if women are willing to race for the love of racing before worrying about the money. "I think if some of the other roadie and mountain bike women came over, they could make it," he says. "You have to create your destiny. If you want to go do it and put the time and energy in and pay your dues, I can't tell you how many years all of the guys did this for no money. And I know the women are still catching up and it's not going to happen overnight."

He also wants to point out the harsh reality: being a bike racer, male or female, is never going to make someone rich. That said, he believes that, "With being creative and getting results and training, the potential is there."

But as Thorne asks and answers: "Is it as much as the men? Probably not. Should it be as much as the men? That's the heated topic. But the reality is that there is no big money."

MO BRUNO ROY ON GETTING SPONSORED

Why aren't more women pro racers? It's simple. "If there's not a way to eat and live racing your bike, it's hard for people to choose that sport," Vareschi notes. And it's even harder as a woman, in smaller fields with less prize money available.

As women, it can be harder to find a team with solid support, and so securing outside sponsors can often prove to be a more financially rewarding option for an elite woman rider. Mo Bruno Roy has some suggestions gleaned from years of understanding how to promote herself and her racing as a product for a brand.

"I think a lot of women aren't looking for individual sponsorship. If they're willing to put the work in that it takes, I think they can get individual sponsorships, but the work it takes is a lot. People think it's too much work and don't have time if they want to train, rest and recover like a real pro. But it is a sacrifice you have to make for a couple of years and it'll happen. It is, honestly, a lot of work.

"A lot of women don't know where to start or what to look at. For me, it was looking at products and brands that I use every day. I wouldn't solicit a company that has products that I wouldn't use. And I went through my cabinets and shelves and looked at what I use every day and in racing. If you look at marketing trends and even just look at magazine ads, a lot of them are featuring women. Women are marketable, they can sell things. And they don't need to be in tight dresses or sexy clothes to do it, women are marketable.

"I think you have to take the initiative to find out what's trending [in marketing] and use it to your advantage and benefit from it. Basically, you're a small business. My taxes say I'm a business, I'm a massage therapist and a cyclist, so I'm going to treat it like a job.

I think a sponsor needs to have a marketing plan that works with using a rider for a reason. I understand that and think it's my job. I work for them, essentially and as someone who's an ambassador for the brand, I think it's your job to represent them as much as possible. So I make myself visible, accessible, available, and probably at the expense of my training a little. But I'm used to that level of energy and I think it's really fun."

While Bruno Roy tends to downplay her stellar results, her strong racing skills are clearly what has propelled her to where she is now, in addition to her marketable personality. And that, Stu Thorne believes, is key for snagging a sponsor. At the end of the day, he says, "You can be the greatest advocate for the brand but you have to back it up with results as well."

Mo Bruno Roy knows how to get—and keep—sponsors. © Pedal Power Photography

9: MAKING IT RUN

"It's not the money that makes me happy; it's not chasing a paycheck around. We want to go out there and make our sponsors happy, but at the end of the day what we really want to do is go out and win races."   –Ryan Trebon

Cyclocross at an elite level in the US wouldn't exist if it wasn't for companies sponsoring teams and individual riders. These companies, cycling-related or otherwise, are the ones who pay for riders to travel, who provide the bikes, components, kit, mechanics, and countless other things that make it possible for riders to race against the best of the best, weekend after weekend.

Companies have been scrambling to get on board and produce cyclocross bikes in all styles, price ranges, and sizes. However, the cyclocross industry is still relatively young. "'Cross bikes used to be an afterthought for companies," Brian Fornes, the marketing man at Raleigh says. "But now, you have carbon 'cross bikes that are down to the weight of pro tour bikes. It's been a pretty dramatic change."

CyclocrossWorld.com was one of the first companies to jump on the cyclocross bandwagon, and just in time. "I've been involved in 'cross since I got into bikes, in 1988," owner Stu Thorne explains. "I bought a mountain bike, raced it all summer and heard about 'cross in New England. I started racing 'cross and did that for a few years. Then, in 1999, we were looking at the sport growing and realized there was no place to get news or products specific to cyclocross. We had brought some products over from Europe and just started selling, and the rest is history."

CyclocrossWorld started as a location for all things 'cross online. "At the onset of CyclocrossWorld, we were the place to get the news and calendars," Thorne says. "We were kind of like what *Cyclocross Magazine* is now, and as 'cross grew, other outlets started doing that too, so we started focusing on the product end of things.

And then, since Thorne was already involved so deeply in the sport, it made sense to start their own team. It started small, as the Cyclocross World team. Then in 2000, Walker Ferguson, Tim Johnson, Jesse Anthony, and Lyne Bessette became part of the team, and as Thorne explains, "One thing really led to another. From a promotional perspective, it's been good having it out there."

Over at Raleigh, "It all started with Single Speed Cyclocross Worlds," Fornes says. "My first 'cross race was single-speed Worlds in Portland. I came back from that and immediately wanted us to make a single speed 'cross bike because I had taken our geared one and just single speeded it out. I asked if we could take the existing frame we had and slap our track dropout on it as a one-off and when that thing hit it just kind of blew up. From there, it kept getting deeper and deeper, farther down the rabbit hole."

And it was just in time, because Raleigh's cyclocross bike line hadn't been doing well, and needed a pick-me up. "In all honesty, we were on the verge of nixing 'cross bikes from our product line. It was mainly because of our poor timing, which most companies in the industry are also guilty of. We'd get our new 'cross bikes done in November, and it was deep into 'cross season, so then they'd have to discount them to get them off the floor before next year's models came out. And then those would show up late. So like other companies, we were struggling with it."

Thankfully, they kept plugging away. "We changed our whole production schedule to try to get them in earlier and earlier," he recalls. "It just took a couple of meetings to convince people we could do well with that stuff, and once we did it, they saw the potential of it. We've always been a huge bike commuter company and once we explained the benefits of 'cross bikes, since they can be used as commuter bikes as well as race bikes, they got it."

Cyclocross bikes have afforded companies the chance to really play with new ideas, since there is no "definite" pattern to a cyclocross bike, and the rules aren't as strict as they are in road. For example, in recent years, cyclocross bike companies are dabbling with the concept of putting disc brakes on cyclocross bikes, and caliper brakes are becoming things of the past. "It's fun," Fornes says, adding that it's also been a learning experience. "We've learned stuff from 'cross bikes that we've transferred to our road bikes. If you look at the chainstays on the carbon bikes, after we fine tuned those, we transferred what we had learned—as far as just being able to absorb some of the shock and abuse that comes from riding in a 'cross race—over to our endurance race bikes. It's been fun in that regard."

Nearly every company sponsors a team: Focus bikes are ridden by the Rapha-Focus team that counts Powers, McDonald and Jones as members, while Cannondale-CyclocrossWorld racers like Johnson, Trebon and Antonneau all obviously ride Cannondales. And Raleigh, while primarily focusing on grassroots teams, has recently started adding a more "pro" element to their teams. "Last year we wanted to get into the pro scene but maintain our grassroots feel," Fornes explains, adding that they want to maintain their level of approachability with our bikes. In order to do that, in 2011, Raleigh hosted the Midsummer Night race where the winners got a contract for a man and woman to "go and live the life of a pro for a year." While the program worked well, they want to take it farther, and now, Fornes says, "We're bringing in a couple of legitimate pros to the program to act like mentors for the two people that we bring in at the race this time. We're still maintaining the grassroots approach but giving these winners the opportunity to get to the USGPs and the Cross after Dark Series and having trainers and mechanics to take care of them."

Companies like Rapha, a "luxury-brand" of cycling clothing, may not make bikes, or cyclocross-specific clothing, but Rapha has taken to cyclocross, and cyclocross has taken to Rapha. Their public relations manager, Slate Olson, explains how they got into supporting 'cross, saying, "I love cyclocross. It's something that is just a fantastic part of cycling and I love its history, its connection to road racing. And being in Portland, seeing the fun that's a part of cyclocross."

He adds, "When I came to Rapha, I brought that along with me. Seeing the opportunity for 'cross to draw attention and grow the sport of cycling in total, it was a natural gateway. There are so many different ways to be a 'cross rider, and it seemed like a great add on to what Rapha was trying to do with the brand and business overall."

It was slow growth at first, as Olson explains. "We made our first 'cross kit and Gary from Independent Fabrication made a bike to match. We just thought it was a cool opportunity to be a part of, and help fuel, the culture and that side of the sport. So that's why we wanted to do it originally."

Rapha was also making a splash within the grassroots scene, and quickly developed the niche of luxury cycling clothing that became popular among the stylish and slightly hip cyclocross scene. "'Cross racers have a lot of style and they're very smart so it wouldn't surprise me that they'd like Rapha," Olson says.

After that, Rapha was in. They wanted to create something in 'cross that paralleled what they already had running on the road. "We've had the Rapha-Condor-Sharp guys racing for six years, and as fans of bike racing, we just wanted something else to be engaged in and excited about when the road season was over. Having a team on any scale really helped us do that, it gave us more stories to tell."

Rapha quickly went from having a team that just looked stylish on the bike, to a team that dominated the national circuit, with Jeremy Powers, Zach McDonald, and Chris Jones all racing in the black and pink kits.

Getting Powers for the 2011 season was a coup even from the beginning, and the Nationals win was icing on the cake. "I've always liked Jeremy.

I didn't know him terribly well, but from a fan's view, he had a great personality. What I was trying to do was have him be part of the three person team we have currently, with Chris Jones and Zach McDonald, who I'd reached out to after they both had great seasons. We knew we wanted to elevate it and that's when we really connected with Jeremy."

Rapha-Focus's Zach McDonald makes his team look good as he heads up the muddy staircase.   © Dejan Smaic

However, Rapha never expected the level of success that they were met with over the course of the season, with not just one National title, but two: the elite men's title and the Under 23 title. "If you'd have told me we'd have two National Champions …" Olson muses, and quickly adds, "Those guys have worked really hard and they deserved that."

Despite being one of the two "big name" teams in the US, with Cannondale-CyclocrossWorld being the other, Olson has reservations about growing too fast. "I'm eager to make sure we're having the same sort of fun and results, and doing so without becoming the Yankees. Everyone hates the Yankees. We can do it our way, and it'll be great.

And as far as the competition between the two big teams, both Olson and Thorne have expressed desire to see another team get guys into the top of the field, so every race doesn't become a Rapha-Focus versus Cannondale-CyclocrossWorld grudge match. "I can't even tell you how highly I think of Stu, I love Tim Johnson, they're all around great people," Olson says. "What I hope will happen is that we have two dominant players so it's like the Giants playing the Patriots every weekend, so it's always going to be a great game and there's always passion behind both camps. And that's not to say that there can't also be another team, like the Jets. And I hope that happens. I don't want it to be just a flip of the coin if it's just going to be Jeremy or Ryan."

Do the teams work for brand recognition? Thorne has a mixed reaction. "It's not as quantifiable or tangible, but a lot of people recognize us from being at the races, and we're just trying to give back to the sport as much as possible," he explains. "So we're there, not just with the big team but with the grassroots team and we sponsor a lot of different programs, like the USGP and local series, like the Alaska cyclocross series. We've helped riders all along the way, we've been part of all that. It's just something I enjoy doing."

For Rapha, it's been purely beneficial, and Olson says, "It's been a fantastic relationship. It's allowed both brands to interact with different mindsets and different markets."

WHAT'S COMING OUT NEXT

"There's not the tradition they have in Belgium. We're running along with whatever we can these days. We're seeing more and more people in the single speed category. We're seeing people racing with flat bars on their bikes, things I've never thought of. The carbon disc bike we're coming out with soon, it's electronic! It's crazy what's coming down the line these days and I like that no one is conforming to any set rules. That's what I like about 'cross. You make your own rules to make sure people are still enjoying it. The sky is the limit right now." –Brian Fornes

10: THE HIJINKS

"There's always a scene going on afterwards. That's one of the differences between here and Europe. It can get a little bigger here but it's still fun for everyone now. The beginners can have fun racing and then have fun watching the pro race. When it becomes more intense and serious like in Europe, it's not the same."

—Luke Keough

Cycling Coverage Gets... Dirty

Get your minds out of the gutter, we're still talking about cyclocross here. If you're a fan of 'cross, or US cyclocross racers specifically, you probably have visited CyclingDirt. The brainchild of Harvard graduate and son of the CyclingNews photographer, Colt McElwaine, CyclingDirt compiles videos of races including live race coverage, post- and pre-race interviews with elite and amateur racers, community-contributed content, and anything that strikes Colt's fancy. His weekly recap show, The Dirt, often takes a turn for the whacky, usually involving some hijinks (in one episode, Colt argues for more 'sexy' men's cycling ads and at the end, starts his own photoshoot session as the camera fades to black). But it's their interviews with racers whom fans know and love that often garner the most attention for their in-depth nature and uncanny ability to reveal the racer's real thoughts on any given race. That, or just showcase a pushup contest between rival racers.

It's the site that you go to when you want to see a racer cry, or when you want to see an interview done entirely with a Christopher Walken accent. It might not always be the pinnacle of serious journalism, but cyclocross isn't the pinnacle of serious racing, even at the highest levels. So the two are a perfect complement to each other.

Websites like CyclingDirt have changed how cycling is seen and spread, even in the past few years. "The most important change is the impact of technology, especially the Internet," veteran 'crosser Pete Webber explains. "Today you can find hundreds of videos on YouTube of Koksijde races. You know the sand is key, you know X, you know Y. One of my favorite sayings is 'proper preparation prevents poor performance.' The Internet has really changed the prep game for the elite international racing."

Cycling Dirt founder Colt McElwaine leaps over course tape to snag the best footage of Ryan Trebon.   © Dejan Smaic

That said, getting live coverage of races is hard, says promoter Joan Hascom. "It's the thing I've grappled with: there's a chicken and egg thing here. You can't get TV coverage on a national level until you can guarantee the network the money, and you can't get the sponsors unless you have a guaranteed TV package." However, thanks to CyclingDirt, she thinks that the tide is turning, and adds, "The Web is a great way to draw people to the sport."

Colt didn't start out as a wanna-be cycling reporter though. Rather, he was a racer-hopeful himself. "I'd been racing mountain bikes forever, and then in 2000 I was at a mountain bike race in the junior race and

Mark McCormack happened to show up at that. We chatted after the race, and he was coaching Jesse Anthony at the time. We exchanged emails, and Mark became my coach. He said, 'Why don't you come try this thing called cyclocross?' and I had never even heard of it. So I went and raced Gloucester for the first time on a borrowed bike. And I said, I'm going to do this from now on."

He was true to his word, but "doing this" didn't necessarily translate to a stellar career as a 'crosser. He says he reached a point, "where I could be a pro and live in the van down by the river or do something else."

It was around this time that inspiration struck. His now-wife, then-girlfriend was a runner, and Colt followed her and her teammates, which led him to a website for running called FloTrack, where they filmed the races and had interviews with the athletes and coaches. Colt says, "I was still racing and training so I fell in love with watching these videos and workouts and hearing people talk about the same stuff I was passionate about. I wasn't in the same sport, but I liked to talk about training."

But FloTrack, owned by FloCast, didn't offer any videos for cycling buffs. Colt didn't think much about it until at a race in Long Island when he was sick and had to skip racing on Day Two. It was his first time simply spectating, and after the race, while talking with the McCormacks and Jesse Anthony, "It just hit me right there."

He thought, "How cool would it be to watch the races and do the interviews?" So, as the story goes, Colt didn't waste any time. "I bought a camera a week later, on Friday night, the night before NBX in Warwick, RI. Didn't race, couldn't sleep all night I was so excited. Got in my car in the morning and drove to Warwick at 4 AM. It was freezing cold, and I filmed 12 hours of footage, filmed every race, all day."

From there, it took off, and fast. "I talked to some friends who knew computer stuff and could make a website, I booked tickets to Worlds and headed to Europe. Along the way, I sent an email to the people who ran FloTrack, saying I'm starting a website just like yours and asked for suggestions. They said, 'That sounds interesting, why don't you fly down to Texas and talk to us about it?' I said, 'ok,' and two months later I flew down, and two days later I flew home with stock options and a website."

He continues, "It wasn't something like, 'I'm going to plan this business out.' In three months it went from not existing to posting videos everyday and traveling everywhere." Now, CyclingDirt has a whole host of contributors and 18 full-time employees.

However, Colt's professional career didn't fare quite as well as CyclingDirt did. "I somehow thought that I was going to go to these races, film everything, have this great website, and race professionally. But I don't think I've raced again since."

He doesn't miss it though. "I still get to do every single bit that I love about it other than the actual racing part. I get to see all the people, ride all the time and talk about bikes."

"I think internet live coverage is the way to do it. For this coming season, we should have 12 weekends of live cyclocross coverage. That from five years ago where you couldn't get results until the Thursday after the race is huge. The sport is seriously professionalized now. It used to be what the MTBers and road guys did to make an extra five grand a year."

And now, people like Colt, who friends and colleagues say sacrifices sleep and food for working on CyclingDirt until the wee hours of the night, are in part responsible for making cyclocross a main focus for some racers: "Now you've got guys like Ryan Trebon and Jeremy Powers and this is how they make their livelihood."

Racers tend to agree, and Geoff Kabush says, "What CyclingDirt's been doing in terms of coverage is doing a great job to build it."

"There's so much more excitement around it. Every year there are new racers and there's more prize money and the fans are enthusiastic. It's more fun when people are more interested in it and you can see a future and you can see it growing," Colt says.

But it's not just about the funny moments, or the race coverage. It's about capturing emotion immediately after races. One of Colt's best moments came from a moment that had every reporter choking back tears…

"It was talking to Jeremy Powers right after he won the National Championship. I think everyone that knows him and is close with him felt like we won something and we were all equally teary-eyed. Of everyone there, everyone wanted to talk to Jeremy, but after he hugged his fiancé, I was the first person who got to talk to him. To see that reaction and be part of that was really cool."

Perhaps the point of CyclingDirt can be summed up by Colt's view of cyclocrossers in the US: "You get the vibe that the people in the US are just having way more fun doing what they're doing. From amateurs all the way to the elites, from the front of the race to the back."

It's Because We're a Family

One of the best parts about cyclocross is that, as Luke Keough puts it, "it's a family affair." Of course, the Keough family knows this more than most, since they even run a family team, Keough Cyclocross. With five brothers, all serious racers, it makes sense to have a team, since training camp can be whenever more than one of them is occupying the Keough homestead. And while the oldest of the brothers has left cyclocross for a bigger career on a road team, United Healthcare, he's still working the pits during his brother's races. And since they have their own pressure washer, it's quite a task.

Luke describes Keough Cyclocross's beginnings as the end of his junior career. "I came out of juniors and we'd already been on a family program run through the shop. I had a lot of opportunities to race for bigger teams all over the world as a junior in 'cross, and I decided to stick with the support I got from family and friends and the shop. And when I got out of juniors I had to decide again, to go for a big team or try to stick around and grow our local scene. My older brother Nick had been riding for Jittery Joes, so we talked to the guy who ran that, got some ideas, and put our own thing together. It's been growing ever since, we want to keep racing together."

The Keoughs aren't the only family who trains together in New England. The Goguens, the Whites and the Curleys have all made New England cyclocross races a veritable family reunion week in and week out during the season. But, as Paul Curley says about racing with his 17-year-old daughter, "The whole family is focused on the season: the diet, the training, the clothes-washing, the bike-cleaning, all of that stuff that goes along with it. It's easier to do it for two people than it is for one."

Twitter, #HeckleMe, and How the Internet Created US 'Cross

"It's about getting the compelling aspects of our sport, what makes it fascinating, which is typically the personalities," promoter Brook Watts claims. "Like the *Behind THE Barriers* kind of stuff. That's how we get new fans."

With the rise of social media like Twitter, the US cyclocross scene developed its niche, fast and furiously. While cyclocross has long been hailed as a friendly, approachable sport even among the elite racers, with Twitter, this was a way to get even closer to the pros that amateurs and fans looked up to. Some racers embraced the trend more than others, and a new culture of cyclocross began to develop. Among the personalities included was Jeremy Powers, who used his online reality show, *Behind THE Barriers*, to show the world what he was like; Adam Myerson, who took on Twitter with guns a-blazin' and never looked back, always making sure that his opinion on all things—especially those cycling-related—was reflected in his Tweets, and being unflinchingly honest in his day-to-day interactions; Tim Johnson, who showed that a pro's Twitter can be engaging with the everyday cyclist; and Molly Cameron, who, similar to Myerson, interacts with the Twitter cycling universe in a way that is absolutely unafraid to tell the truth.

US racers don't just come out to race; they come out to cheer (and heckle)!   © Pedal Power Photography

As Cameron says, "What's cool about cyclocross is that you have a lot of accessibility to individual personalities. I think the three of us [Myerson, Powers, Cameron] are really, really serious and we're all at totally different levels in the sport, but we don't take ourselves too seriously."

In terms of taking oneself seriously, no one has done a better job at poking fun at herself that mountain biker turned cyclocrosser Georgia Gould. When her season wasn't going according to plan, she invented her own Twitter campaign, the hashtag #heckleme. Since heckling is as much a part of cyclocross as barriers are, the campaign was an immediate success—and a laugh riot. Hecklers from all over the country were jeering at racing and across the Internet, and while Gould's results may not have improved by much, her great attitude about the season kept people in her corner and rooting for her.

What is happening through all of this, Cameron says, is, "We can laugh at ourselves and we don't mind putting ourselves out there and having a good time but are really serious and race really hard. And there are not a lot of people who do that. There are other people who are fun and funny but don't put themselves out there as much."

And the social media has done more than just promote the personalities, Mark Vareschi adds. "Social media allowed the sport to take off and allowed access to the personalities in the sport. And it's part of what keeps cyclocross quirky. We have these personalities, and they race well. They're evangelical about the sport, they've invested deep in the sport. It's how we tell our story."

The worry though, it seems, is that, "If you're too funny, in a way you're de-legitimizing yourself as an athlete." Perhaps that's why, Cameron postulates, "Road racing can be pretty serious, and there aren't a lot of funny riders out there. Everyone is kind of an automaton." But in cyclocross, at no point are the riders listed above putting on a show, or acting out of character.

"I think it's just our personalities too," Cameron says. "We do it how we do it. It's a head-game."

Prize Tattoo: Single Speed Cyclocross World Championships

Single-speeders are a breed of their own in cyclocross. While some races have single speed categories, more often than not the racers race in their respective categories with the handicap of having just one gear. However, there is one time of year when single-speeders take center stage.

Murphy Mack is one of the promoters who was tasked with arguably the most difficult job in cyclocross: making Single Speed Cyclocross World Championships (SSCXWC) into the spectacle that it is today. What got him into promoting? Actually, that very thing: he was looking for some kind of excitement in a race. "I was looking at all of the races in the area and they seemed very formulaic. Things needed to be freshened up a little bit; I saw no variety and wanted to add some unique twists to things." Enter SSCXWC. "It's so off the wall and the people who race in it are a breed apart. They're 1,000% committed (some should be as well) to the sport and they're in it for the love of the game, not the UCI points. SSCXWC is the pinnacle of "Give me everything you've got!" racing." And yes, the winner is (in theory) given the prize of a SSCXWC tattoo, and yes, they can get it with the crowd watching. It's no surprise that so far, SSCXWC has been a West Coast tradition, since that side of the country is seemingly more dedicated to preserving the more party-oriented, culturally, side of cyclocross. Three cities later, and it's still going strong. First up was a stop in Oregon. Mack explains, "Since it began in Portland the crowd was a bunch of nutball hyper-dedicated CX racers to begin with. They wanted a more-fun/less-serious (read: no angry, stiff, stuffy UCI officials) event where that special breed of Portland rider can really be themselves." Mission accomplished, the mayhem moved North to Washington state. "Seattle, where the sun doesn't shine, had their hands on the big party race and really threw themselves into it. They created a wild, fun and crazy course that reset the bar for the next city to get it." And then, it came to Mack's hometown: "When we got it for San Francisco, we knew we had something special that we needed to not only make grow, but we had to take what the previous years had done and make it even more over the top and bigger than life. We had the crowd and the city to do it with too, and we knew it."

The tradition of craziness continued, and between a pond of filth that racers essentially swam through with their bikes, and the gold bikini and speedo that winners Julie Krasniak and Chris Jones donned post-race,

Mack can rest peacefully knowing that he helped carry on a tradition that will hopefully make 'crossers proud for years to come.

© Pedal Power Photography

Beer Gardens, Breweries, and Dollar Hand-Ups

Cyclocross and beer go hand-in-hand. Case in point: Nationals in Bend, Oregon, were held at the Deschutes Brewery. Not enough proof? Just visit any major race, from the Shimano Series to the USGPs and look for where the crowd is cheering the loudest. Congratulations, you just found the beer garden.

Beer might just be the key for growing cyclocross as a spectator sport in the US. As Nicole Duke says, "The beer brings in a whole lot of culture. We're going to be a traveling circus."

And beer leads to antics, like dollar bill hand-ups. "Let's go back to the dollar bill grabbing, which is what the Belgians call what we do. Where the heck did that come from?" Brook Watts asks. "Any given day you catch me, I'm a fan of it or I totally hate it, and I'll tell you that thank goodness in Europe the smallest paper denomination is the five pound note, because that would go crazy in Europe. But there, you're not going to throw a pound coin."

Hijinks like dollar handups to pros at the barriers might be less than professional, but at the same time, it's what makes the sport uniquely American.

Not a sport for the faint of heart.   © Pedal Power Photography

11: A BEGINNER'S GUIDE TO CYCLOCROSS

"You're racing each other but you're racing yourself, and there's that battle inside your head with when to suffer and if you should chase that next person down, your feet are numb, your hands are cold, you're feeling crappy ... but you do it because it's cross and wimps don't race cross."
— Katie Compton

You can race 'cross at any age, from kiddie 'cross to the masters, like National Champion Julie Lockhart does. © Pedal Power Photography

The Gear

"We used to stock all of these 26" skinny tires for the person who wanted to convert a mountain bike to go race 'cross and we don't stock that stuff anymore. You can go out and buy a $1,000 'cross bike to get started. That's changed dramatically over the years. The amount of product and quality of product out there is phenomenal."
—Stu Thurne

Thanks to the growth of the sport, cyclocross bikes have become infinitely easier to come by, and that, according to Andrew Yee, has made a major difference to the sport. "It's grown in participation and it's grown tremendously in equipment options. It's also grown in dollars and stature. I can't emphasize enough how dramatic the changes in equipment have become," he says. "Before, we would all cobble together bikes from old touring bikes or road frames, and eventually hybrids. Now, every manufacturer has five to ten cyclocross models and now we're talking disc brakes and cyclocross wheels and 50 different tires available on the market."

A cyclocross bike may resemble a road bike, at first glance, but there are quite a few subtle differences that make it difficult to simply take a road bike and remake it into a cyclocross bike. The first and most readily apparent difference is the tires. While road bikes use thin, slick tires, a 'cross bike uses tires that are the same width (or a little bigger) but covered in knobs, similar to the treads found on mountain bike tires. These treads are what allow the wheels to grip and get through mud, fight its way over roots, and hang on to grass in corners. The less obvious difference in tires is the pressure that one typically runs. On a road bike, tires are run at around 100 PSI. On a 'cross course, tires usually are run much lower, between 20 and 50 PSI, depending on the course and the rider's weight and personal preference.

Aside from tires, there are other intrinsic differences. Gearing tends to be different, since 'cross has sections similar to mountain bike courses that require more quick pedaling, and pedaling over grass or dirt automatically requires more power per pedal stroke. Additionally, forks need to be wider in order to allow for the wider width of the tires. Caliper brakes are used, though disc brakes are slowly becoming more and more popular with the cyclocross set. The technology, like in road and mountain biking, is constantly changing, though cyclocross remains one of the more "purist" sports, with gear tending to stay more traditional. In fact, top pros like Katie Compton argue strenuously against their use. "The thing with discs is that you never need to stop in cross. If you're racing it, you need to slow, you need to check your speed but you never need to stop," Compton says.

That traditional, less innovation-focused, approach has created an interesting group of racers, with a wide variety of bikes. Perhaps one of the best parts about racing cyclocross is that it's an easily accessible sport, gear-wise. You can show up in the lower categories with an old mountain bike, or even just a hybrid, and still complete the race and have a blast doing it. However, if you do get serious about racing, cyclocross bikes can range from lower level (around $500) to upwards of $5,000.

When picking the bike, the best thing you can do is find your local bike shop that stocks multiple options for 'cross bikes, ask a lot of questions, and test various bikes out. Racer and Coach Adam Myerson has some suggestions when it comes to picking out a bike: "It depends on if you're coming from road or mountain biking but I think the key is getting something tall enough that you can get your bars as high as you need them and you can sit up."

The key difference is that, as he explains, "It's not road position. You need to sit in your saddle and take weight off of your hands if you need to steer, as opposed to road position where you're bent over and have to support yourself. Driving on a road bike is much different than driving on a 'cross bike."

And racer Ryan Trebon's best training advice is actually bike advice, though not about fit. His top tip? "Learn how to ride your bike. Be comfortable. Most people are too stiff, they don't know how the bike feels to ride at the limit. Most people don't focus on riding, they focus on intervals and stuff. But then people don't know how to handle their bikes."

So when you get a 'cross bike, be sure to ride it. Ride it on the 'cross course, the trails, and throw on slicks and do your intervals on it instead of a road bike. The familiarity with how the bike handles in every condition will only enhance your bike racing.

DO YOU NEED A 'CROSS BIKE? (AND HOW TO GET ONE)

According to cyclocross coach Chris Mayhew, getting a cyclocross bike shouldn't be your top priority when you start racing.

"I think you can absolutely race without one; I think the sport has improved so much it's ridiculous how it's changed. There used to not be cyclocross bikes. I started on a mountain bike; plenty of people started on a MTB. If it's your first race, having an MTB is the least of your worries. It's better to do the race at all, rather than waiting because you need to save up for one. Get in the sport and worry about the details as they come. We've even had women attend clinics on road bikes."

However, if you've raced a few times and are ready to commit, you still don't need to drop thousands of dollars on a bike right off the bat.

"There's a lot of really good used equipment out there, so pay attention to what's being sold. People tend to not hold on to stuff as long these days. Look at the 'Cyclocross Magazine' forums, look immediately after Nationals online, and look right before the season as well. Do a season on what you have, and then when you get an idea of what bike you want, start looking for those as they go up for sale. Buying a used bike is definitely the way to go at first."

Even with all the right gear, you will still crash sometimes. © Pedal Power Photography

The Training

Training for cyclocross is unlike training for road cycling or mountain biking in that it has several components:

- Power/Speed
- Technical Handling
- Running/Carrying

Getting into cyclocross is perhaps easier than getting started as a road rider or a mountain biker: for one thing, the bikes are available in a wide price range, and even the low level models are fine for a first year racer. Additionally, as a newbie to cycling, a cyclocross bike is ideal for commuting in all kinds of weather, and riding on the road or on the dirt.

Racing cyclocross is also more newbie-friendly than the other disciplines. Luke Keough says that the best part for him is that, "It's relatively easy to do at any level. You're always racing someone, that's what I tell people.

If you're a Cat 3/4, the Masters guy who's out for fun, you're always racing someone, there's always someone in front or behind you that you're trying to beat inside the race. You challenge yourself and that's one of the biggest draws that there is. It can be a personal challenge or it can be a race for the win. It's fun and competitive at the same time."

If you're working a normal 9-5 job, have family constraints, or just plain aren't ready for a major time commitment, cyclocross is also a great starting point. Mary McConneloug is happy to point out that, "It is a feasible sport to incorporate into a life while managing a full time job and family. To train right for cyclocross requires far less time since the race is 45 minutes to an hour long. It really only requires about 10 to 15 hours a week to train and prepare fitness to be ready to race."

Even if you've been a MTB-er or a road racer for years, expect to still face a learning curve. Ryan Trebon reminds us that, "Good mountain bikers don't always make good 'cross racers just like road racers don't always make good 'cross racers. It's a different dynamic on the bike so you just need to practice." And that's why, he says, "I tell people to just get comfortable pushing the bike around. You don't just treat it like a road bike, you have to really work the bike."

As courses in the US strive to appeal to every level of racing, some of the more "gnarly" aspects of courses are being removed, much to racers like Todd Wells' dismay. For mountain bikers, the "grass crit" style of cyclocross racing is a major detriment, since they aren't as equipped with an aerobic engine as a road racer might be. "As cyclocross has become more UCI-focused in the US, the courses have become more sterile," Wells says. "We used to have crazy obstacles, tons of barriers and all sorts of skill-based riding. The season also used to start later so it seemed like bad weather was more prevalent and bike handling was more important."

If you're new to the sport and looking to find a coach, just take a peak at the top of the pro field. Elite riders often act as coaches to make ends meet and to hone their skills. Katie Compton is one of the most well known examples. Rather than coaching herself, she selects the occasional athlete to take under her wing, and her husband, Mark Legg Compton, does the same. Compton started coaching almost by accident in college: "I needed an internship to finish my degree in Exercise Science at the University of Delaware. My dad found a coaching internship through Carmichael Training Systems. I moved out to Colorado, and that four month internship turned into six months and that turned into a year and a permanent job. Then I started working on my own as a contract coach. I'm not coaching nearly as much as I used to, I used to coach full-time, just to pay the bills. I coach a little now to stay in the game and have something else to do, someone else's training to think about. I like to help out younger riders who can't afford coaching."

Compton's best free coaching advice? "Technically, I think making sure you're smooth on and off the bike is where you can save a lot of time and energy. So that would be something to practice until you have it down perfectly, or at least as perfect as you can get it. For fitness, short, hard intensity. Sprint work, fast accelerations. Because 'cross isn't a sustained effort. I think some people forget that it's a 40 minute race [or an hour for elite men] but you're never doing tempo. You're doing above or below but never a sustained effort."

Planning Your Season

Most 'crossers, from the top pros to the first timers, are involved in some other sport during the year, whether it's road racing, mountain biking or even triathlon. So rather than just focusing on training for cyclocross all year 'round, there is a balancing act of sorts that needs to happen.

For some, like Geoff Kabush, cyclocross is a means to an end, a way of training while still being competitive. "I always did something in the fall, because to shut down racing in September makes for a long winter, so to stay fit, it's always fun to have something else to do in the fall. 'Cross lets me keep riding my bike and stay relatively fit until I have to get back to training for mountain bike season."

Even Kabush is susceptible to the cyclocross-cycle though. When racing 'cross, especially in heavily race-populated areas like the East Coast or Northwest, it's tempting to race two days a week, every week. With that much intensity, it can be easy to overtrain. To avoid this pitfall, Kabush has these words of wisdom: "Get as fit as you can before the season starts, especially when you're racing a full season, because it's basically just racing and resting. The biggest mistake is people try to train too much, and it's maybe good to not race every single weekend. But it's tempting, because racing is so much fun. But racing twice a week isn't great for building fitness."

And if it's your first season, Luke Keough cautions that you may not see immediate results. But there is light at the end of the tunnel, if the tunnel is your second (or third) season. "My best advice is just sticking with what you're doing. Training is an accumulation of work over a period of time. That's the mathematical, practical description of it. It's true that it may not pay off for a year or two, but it will."

He continues on to say, "Everyone wants instant results, that's the way the world is, everyone wants something now, done right away. But as far as training goes, you can't expect quick changes and quick results but they will come if you stick to a good program. So it's not necessarily a 'do this' or 'do that,' it's about sticking with a solid program. Whatever that program is. It'll pay off in the future, maybe not this year, but in later seasons."

Mo Bruno Roy echoes Keough's advice. "Have patience," she cautions. "There seems to be a time warp in people's minds. For the amount of work they've been putting in, they seem to want results to be so much more than they are. This is my tenth year racing a bike and I feel like in the last two years, my body is finally getting it. It took this long because before then I felt like every season I was starting all over again, and now I'm developing muscle memory. My body is starting to remember cycling."

She continues: "So it is a test of patience. The results are not immediate, and whether goals are weight loss or fitness or results, it takes twice as long as you expect." Then why do it? "Ultimately you need to be trying to have fun. Especially if you're not at a pro level. If you're not having fun, then what are you doing? There are too many other fun things to do than torturing yourself doing something you think is going to make you happy at some point if you spent all this time being miserable. It has to be intense and serious to be fulfilling but there has to be an element of fun."

Getting impatient? Stu Thorne suggests not committing to just one thing. "Getting into it is hard but as you get into it, mix it up," he says. "Go do a mountain bike race, go do a crit, go do a road race. I think it's good in general to mix it up and keep it interesting because it's pretty easy to get burned out."

And of course, Pete Webber is quick to remind new racers that a day off isn't the end of the world, or your season. "You will get sick at least once during the season and probably miss a whole week. Don't worry about it."

Getting Started

So you bought a cyclocross bike and plan to start racing on it. Now what? The first step is simple, says Myerson. "Ride your 'cross bike all the time." This means, he explains, "Using road wheels when you're on the road, and do all of your interval training in the grass, in the dirt. Group 'cross workouts are hugely beneficial, you get the group dynamic, you get to drive your bike. And early in my career, the thing that benefitted me the most was going on these mountain bike rides on a 'cross bike. It teaches you how to ride, how to pick good lines. Plus, it's just fun."

Paul Curley has been racing for a long time: certainly long enough to offer some sage advice for new racers, considering he spent his formative years training racers like Adam Myerson and, later, Jeremy

Powers. "For someone getting into cyclocross, they really need to spend a lot of time riding their bike in difficult conditions," he says. "There's no way you can go out and expect to do well in a muddy race if you haven't spent a lot of time in muddy races. Cyclocross is a sport that takes a very long time to learn."

Whether you're new to bike racing in general or cyclocross in specific, 'cross has so many small components to it, and it is nearly impossible to demonstrate these skills in a text, no matter how long or involved. In order to properly be introduced to cyclocross, the simplest way is to find a local practice. A coach from JBV Coaching, Chris Mayhew, has been racing and coaching for nearly twenty years, and his first suggestion for newcomers to the sport was that, "If you're new to cyclocross, you need to find your local cyclocross practice." Why? "It's a specific skill set involved in cyclocross that isn't in other disciplines. Barriers, carrying your bike; you're going to learn those at the local clinic course or practice."

Depending on your location, that may be easier said than done, but putting on a practice is simple enough: find several like-minded friends, or visit a race in order to find these men and women, check out a local race or two to get a general sense of the courses, and then, get to it.

"Everything follows once you can find a local clinic or practice," Mayhew says. And as for the friends you ride with, look for people at your same level of dedication. If you want to enjoy yourself, look for more casual racers, but if you're serious about racing, Mayhew suggests that you need to find "guys to train with who want to ride hard during the season."

If you're starting from scratch, with a local practice that you're going to have to develop on your own, Mayhew suggests bringing in an expert to get the groundwork started and show your crew the basics. Look for a local pro, or if there's enough interest, bring one in. Don't be intimidated by having to start your own practice even if you've never raced before. "Everyone has to start somewhere, at some point there wasn't a cyclocross practice."

© Pedal Power Photography

Mark Vareshi agrees with Mayhew, and since he's responsible for starting the six-time collegiate conference championship team that is Rutgers University Cycling, he's seen his share of new racers. He suggests, "Seek out a weekly practice where people know more than you. Like, really know more than you and have been doing it for a long time, because they can teach you a lot of stuff."

Top skills to practice at a clinic? "Starts, dismounts, remounts, and carries," Mayhew suggests.

The clinic can also morph into a race simulation. "I tell people to focus their week around doing a super hard mock-race on Wednesday," Pete Webber says. "Riding your 'cross bike really fast on realistic terrain with fun training partners is the best way to get better. That's why we have the Wednesday Worlds in Boulder. I've been helping lead that group for almost 20 years and it's helped develop a lot of really fast racers."

In its early days, racing cyclocross was a simple matter of grabbing whatever bike was available to you and riding or running it around a field. Now, the game has changed. "Everyone is faster. That is the thing across the board that I've noticed. And how much better everyone's technique is. I think a lot of it has to do with the opportunities to attend coaching clinics. Adam Myerson has been at the vanguard of that, but everyone has caught on," Vareschi says. "Most people know the proper technique to get on and off the bike even if they can't execute it. With the advent of online coaching, people are just faster even in a straight line."

Learning Technique

"Practice dismounting and remounting the correct way until you get it dialed," says Mark McCormack. It's his best suggestion for a new rider. And it won't be easy.

There is no magical formula for learning cyclocross technique. It simply takes practice, repetition, and hopefully learning from someone smarter than yourself. To that end, signing up for a local clinic or attending a weekly practice can be invaluable.

"Like any sport, repetition is key," Amy Dombroski says. "Remounts, dismounts, you can be totally terrible at them or you can make them look like artwork. The guys in Europe and some of the guys here, you watch them and it's just so fluid."

And if you're new to the sport of cycling and are still working to develop your fitness, technique practice can be a good break from the tough interval workouts and more aerobically based rides. "I think that's something that doesn't take a lot of fitness, it's going out and doing it and repeating, repeating, repeating," Dombroski explains. "It's like baseball with practicing your swing. I think finding the right person to show you how to do it and then doing repeats of it is important."

Mary McConneloug's explanation of why technique is important speaks to the idea of poetry in cycling: "It is important to be smooth in transitions, getting off and on the bike. When you have mastered it, it sort of feels like a dance with your bike. When racing and pushing anaerobic thresholds it can be tough to finesse the right moves. Getting to know your bike and how to handle it on a run up, how to get on and off quickly and seamlessly. Mastering this can save you time and energy if you are quick and efficient."

Stu Thorne has helped develop athletes for over 20 years, and for him, once a rider gets started, "If you start to get into it a little more, then I'd say getting the technique down is key." To that end, he suggests that a racer, as Myerson says, stays on the 'cross bike all Fall. Additionally, he recommends "going to 'cross practice once a week, and doing efforts along the way in your training." Those efforts, he explains, make all the difference. "You need to do those explosive efforts so you can maintain. 'Cross is just putting out explosive amounts of energy, recovering for a second and doing it again, for 40 minutes [an hour for elite men]."

And if you can't stand the monotony of training alone, or get bit by the competition bug, Thorne suggests, "Doing criteriums in the summer helps, especially if you don't just sit on the back. Racing a mountain bike is huge too, since technique and handling is such a huge part of racing 'cross. If you can have a little mountain bike background, you'll get the handling thing even better."

Of course, learning technique for 'cross isn't exactly simple. "The cyclocross remount is difficult to explain," Pete Webber says. "How does a person leap skyward into the saddle without causing serious damage 'down under'? There is only one way to learn this elusive skill—spend some time watching an experienced crosser do it and then go practice it yourself about a thousand times."

© Dejan Smaic

When asked for the best training advice for a new racer, Geoff Proctor waxes philosophical and quotes Aristotle. "We are what we repeatedly do. Excellence is not an act, but a habit."

He explains further, thankfully, saying, "In the classroom, in cyclocross, we are what we repeatedly do. It's not some stroke of luck, it becomes habitual. So I'm all about building the toolbox for these guys I coach. You have to look at races, be in races, figure out what tools you need to succeed at this sport."

Proctor thinks that the first step to developing technique is understanding which techniques need developing. It's not all about the remount/dismount combination. "There's so much that goes into it, the mental and the technical, that you've got to figure out those skills and you've got to practice them. For instance, bunny hopping. It's been interesting seeing that skill develop."

He continues, "Now, as a young rider, you've got to learn how to hop some things. That would be my best tip. Train so you're ready for anything. Races in the US are less technical in general, and in Europe you'll see things you won't see here, so you need to develop those skills and be ready for them."

Learning proper foot placement in dismounting is key. © Pedal Power Photography

Of course, technique isn't just about barriers, bunnyhopping, remounting or dismounting. Sure, those are the important cyclocross skills to master, but what about the "simple" things, like riding in the mud, on off-cambers, through tight turns, in the grass, in the gravel, and over roots? Newbie racers sometimes make the mistake of not trying out their bike on different terrain, and when they get into a race that isn't set up exactly like their local practice course, they're at a loss. McCormack suggests that a newbie should, "Work on cornering speeds in a variety of surfaces like grass, sand, and leaves."

To work on more broad-range technical skills, racers suggest the obvious: get on a mountain bike. If you don't have one, take your 'cross bike to the nearest non-technical (or at least, not extremely technical) mountain bike course, and ride in the woods. Laura Van Gilder says, "The biggest thing is to just ride your bike. If you don't have technical skills, if you don't have a mountain bike background at all, get out on a mountain bike and feel what that's like. They're different sports, but that's where you can get those technical skills."

Jeremy Powers shows how the pros have adopted the habit of bunny-hopping barriers during races.   © Dejan Smaic

Myerson tends to agree, adding, "Learning how to pick your way through a rocky trail on a 'cross bike without flatting will make you a better racer." So if you don't have a mountain bike, don't discount trail riding. Rather, look at it as a situation that you can use to your advantage. As an added bonus, this time in the woods can count as your endurance ride: "Keeping your skills sharp, doing endurance rides in the woods instead of on the road is a fun way of keeping the intensity up without mentally having to focus on it, while working on skills at the same time."

At the end of the day, thanks to the slightly more beginner-friendly nature of courses in the US, learning technique, while important, might not be the make-it-or-break-it factor in your races anymore, as a lot of pros have cautioned. "Everyone puts a lot of importance on mounting and dismounting because you have to be able to do that. But they aren't the most important skills anymore," Myerson notes. "They were when we had six or eight dismounts per lap and how quick you could get on or off your bike was actually really important."

Now, "Pedaling is what matters most in 'cross." Myerson believes that the most important technique to master is "your ability to make as much power as possible riding across a muddy, bumpy field. Applying power across uneven terrain is actually the most important technique in 'cross. From there, being able to turn well, to determine exit and entrance speeds, to pick good lines. Pedaling and turning."

Sounds simple, but to do so at high speeds becomes trickier. And Myerson will never say that proper barrier technique is unimportant anymore: "You do have to practice it though. Even now, you can't complete a lap of a 'cross course without being able to do that."

All About the Run

As coach and cyclocross fanatic Pete Webber says, "Running is what sets cyclocross apart—you must embrace it no matter how much you hate it."

When Paul Curley explains cyclocross to someone, he says, "I always say it's a cross between road racing and mountain bike racing with a little bit of running thrown in." However, he's quick to add that, "in all the years I've been racing, I've never done run-specific training. I don't think it's a runner's sport. You get guys who are good runners, but they weren't runners, they were bike racers who happen to have the physique to be good runners. Cyclocross is a cycling event. It's not a running event."

Running as prep for cyclocross is one of the most controversial topics when it comes to training. Courses vary and in some areas and some races, a rider can get away with almost no running, other than over the barriers. But for some muddier races, or races with short, steep hills, running is part and parcel of the whole racing experience. If you came to the sport with a background in running, likely no further training is required. But if you're new to running, you may need to do some run practice in order to improve your race.

Sometimes you can ride the sand. Other times, you can't, so you run as fast as you possibly can and hope that no one else can ride it.   © Pedal Power Photography

Mayhew agrees, saying that, "Running is such a controversial thing in cyclocross. People are all over the board."

As a coach, Mayhew isn't a devotee to running. "I'd say I'm at one end where I deemphasize running. Include it during cyclocross practice but I don't think you need to run 30 minutes a week. You're running at a much higher speed than you would for 20-30 minutes."

Adam Myerson tends to agree with Mayhew, but adds that, "You should run enough that the running you do in the race doesn't injure you. And that's it." While some people believe that running can make or break a race, he's of the mindset that, "Very few races are won in the running, especially in the US. Occasionally we get a muddy race with some threshold running, but you just want to run enough so you're capable of doing it."

Furthermore, he simply doesn't see it as a skill that can be honed to perfection. Rather, he believes, "Running is like sprinting: you're a runner, or you're not; you're a sprinter, or you're not. You can improve it so it doesn't injure you and doesn't slow down other parts of your power. So jogging during the week for adaptive purposes is all you need to do."

Cross Training of the Other Variety

In cyclocross, there's more to racing than keeping the rubber side down on your bike. On any given course, Myerson points out, "You need to be able to pick your bike up and carry it, and sort of run with it on your back, and you have to be able to ride just out of your saddle, so there's a lot of core strength involved with being able to ride your bike not sitting in the saddle."

And that's where core training comes in. He doesn't think a lot is necessary, just the basics: "You can do that with sit-ups, pushups, and back extensions, and that's efficient for what you need."

Chris Mayhew agrees but believes a more efficient method is combining flexibility training with the core work. "I'm not a big fan of weight, but I am a really big fan of some sort of yoga or pilates. It's great because it includes a lot of stretching and some core. That's critical for success in cyclocross, so I'd encourage some balancing activity on your off day to work out the kinks."

Your First Race

Stu Thorne has advice for new racers, and they might not want to hear it: "You'd better be ready to suffer. You have to have that ability to endure half an hour of complete pain. You can't really train for that."

Fair warning: "It's going to be really chaotic; it's going to go really fast," Mayhew says. Aside from that, "It's going to hurt more than you thought it would, and you're also going to really, really enjoy it. And you'll learn all the things you didn't realize that you didn't know."

Learning the right line to take is key. Following a pro in a warmup lap is a great way of finding the right lines.   © Pedal Power Photography

Rather than packing up the car and heading out alone to go race, Mayhew suggests the buddy system. "Don't roll solo," he says. And when you hit the road, "allow plenty of time to get there. Several hours. More than you would for a road race because you want to warm up on the course."

When you're packing, take the "more is more" approach and bring everything except for (and maybe even including) the kitchen sink. Mayhew's suggestion is simply to "Bring everything you own. Don't look at the weather; just bring everything you own. You never know what the weather is going to be, and it might change as the days go on. The first race might be freezing, later in the day it could be moderate."

Speaking of freezing weather, Pete Webber has a tip of his own, and again, new racers may not like it: "Resistance is futile—you can try to stay warm but you will fail."

At the course, the best part about racing cyclocross is the approachability of the pros. Because they race on the same course that you do, typically you can catch a few of them out pre-riding earlier in the day. Pre-riding gives you a chance to see the entire course and know what you're up against. Mayhew's best advice is to, again, use the buddy system. "When you get there, find someone more experienced, follow them around the course, to registration, be their little duckling. That's the great thing about the sport: if Powers is going to do a lap, you can do a lap with him."

Learning to Suffer

One of the key differences between cyclocross and road racing is that cyclocross, while tactical, isn't quite as tactic-driven as a road race is. There aren't many opportunities for drafting or soft-pedaling, and more often than not, it's an all-out effort as soon as the gun goes off. To that end, racer Laura Van Gilder says that for training, her best advice is riding hard, and, "Teaching your body to suffer in that capacity."

At the end of the day, the simplest advice for a new racer came from Molly Cameron: "As bike racers, I realize we're always looking for excuses. As bike racers, we want to quantify everything. And adapt. And attack it. And figure out how to take it on. Stop looking for excuses and just race your bike."

Post race cleanup: use whatever you can to get the mud off you and your rig. © Pedal Power Photography

© Pedal Power Photography

With Kiddie Cross races at nearly every major 'cross race in the US, the temptation to get 'em started young can be hard to combat. At nearly every kid's event, ranging from two-and-three-year-olds racing to the 15-16 Junior races, parents can be heard around the course screaming what they believe to be encouragement to kids. But really, what happens more often, is that it burns out junior riders before they even have the chance to reach their full potential. Kaitie Antonneau has a suggestion for those juniors, and for their parents:

"I think you need to have fun doing it. For me, I just had fun doing it until I was sixteen, and then I started to really understand that I'm training, I'm doing this because "why," it's going to make me better "why," and up until then, my parents never pushed me. You need to have fun up until a certain point, and if you want to do it and you want to be successful then you can go for it. There's just so many years you can do it, and I see a lot of kids get burned out on it because their parents are pushing them."

If your son or daughter is interested in pursuing a career in cyclocross, though, take advantage of the developmental programs that are out there. Geoff Proctor runs EuroCrossCamp for youngsters with serious 'cross talent, most races have junior fields, and all over the county, Kiddie Cross Clinics are popping up. Jeremy Powers got his start young, and offers these suggestions for budding pros:

"If you're a junior, make sure you're showcasing yourself in front of whatever team you want, or in front of USA Cycling, or whoever it is you want to notice your talent. Make sure you seize that opportunity."

He continues, "When I was 16, I got invited to the National Team Camp for mountain biking, and that's a Talent I.D. camp where they have a mini race series. For me it was short track, uphill time trial and cross country, and they did VO2Max testing. I had decent VO2Max and won the short track and uphill time trial. If you win, you're supposed to go on to the Olympic training center. I never got there. Looking back on that, a lot of the guys that went there didn't end up making it. In retrospect, it's not bad that I didn't make it to the training center. But at the time, I was angry about it. And when Team Devo and John Kemp came along, they gave me an opportunity. Tons of great riders came through that team, some of the best riders in the country came from that program. If it wouldn't have been for that program, I wouldn't be where I am today."

Moral of the story? If your young racer is interested, make sure they look at all of the resources available, from training camps to developmental teams. But if your young racer just wants to ride his or her bike, don't push. Like in Kaitie Antonneau's case, that talent and drive will come naturally if you don't force it.

"I feel like this is a sport where someone can't make you do it. Your parents can't make you go out and train, and do intervals and stuff like that. I've never really wanted to not race my bike. I've experienced what happens when you cheat in your training, and I've learned from it. And you can take what you've learned from it and do it again.

-Kaitie Antonneau

"Do everything that you're not good at, all the time. There's no sense training at the things that you're good at, you need to focus on the things that you're not good at and make those weak points your strong points. Because that's ultimately what will make you a better rider." -Jeremy Powers

GOING PRO

Katie Compton should be a rock star in the sport. She should be on the cover of not just *Cyclocross Magazine* or *Bicycling*, but *Sports Illustrated.* However, Compton has learned the hard way that this is a sport you do for love, not because you expect to make a lot of money doing it. However, if you want to go pro, she has some suggestions:

- Pick up golf? If you want to make money doing sports, I wouldn't recommend cycling. It's hard to make money and have a consistent paycheck and get the respect that you've earned from working hard, from being entertainment and winning races. Cycling in general, it's hard to make money. So I think what you have to do is have an education, first and foremost. And then, follow your love and try not to go into debt doing it.
- Pick and choose your races. Pick the ones you're going to do well in. Save your money. Make the good ones count, don't spread yourself too thin. Get good results so you can find those sponsors and get that support. That's what it comes down to. Come with your A game.

- It's such a hard, unforgiving sport. There's so much more disappointment than there is success. I question why I do this shit all the time, too. But I love this sport, that's why I'm doing it. Cycling is such a huge part of my life, it's something I was going to do regardless. I just don't want to get to the point where I hate doing it, because it's something I've loved for 25 years of my life.

Mark McCormack adds in his two cents: "Set your personal goals and go after them. If you want to be a top US racer, race in the US. If you want to be a top global racer, move to Europe and race in Europe."

You can do all the training, but crashes happen. Just laugh about it afterwards.
© Pedal Power Photography

12: THE FUTURE OF 'CROSS

"There's more media, more opportunities. It's grown considerably every year since I've been in it. The way people watch the races, view the sport, view us as racers... it's all changing. Spectators, bike sales, everything."
–Jeremy Powers

With Worlds coming to the US this year and USA Cycling declaring that cyclocross is the fastest growing sport in the country, what does the future hold for the sport?

© Pedal Power Photography

For race promoters, the future looks bright. As Adam Myerson notes, "By definition, we're limited by how many races you can run in a single day and how many racers you can fit on a course within that race. And you can see Cross Crusades are already maxing that out." Not a bad problem to have, though it certainly does bring up an interesting point about if and how series in the US are to continue growing, and at what point the nature of what a race day looks like will need to change. Some promoters believe the answer is to create two series: one with pro races, held on a different course, and on a similar, nearby course, host the amateur races. But ultimately, any growth is good growth at this point in the game, as long as cyclocross in the US stays true to its roots.

Most of the elite racers think that Worlds in the US will be a game-changer. For one thing, there's a mandatory clause that it needs to be televised, presenting the first chance to make a push for races to be watched, and popularized. The accessibility and relative safety of the sport as compared to road or mountain biking could be a determining factor in the sport's popularity in the future. Tim Johnson highlights these key points and says, "I see a lot of television coverage, I see a kids 'cross race and series at every high school around the country to take place on school grounds. There's nothing better than 'cross because it can fit in any school year. I think that there's going to be a true leading series of races that are a legit National series that all the best riders from every region go to."

With Worlds coming to the US, the biggest discussion is that of television time. In order to host Worlds, the race must be live-broadcast, and will be the first major attempt at broadcasting a race in the US, outside of online live race feeds. This is a chance for cyclocross to get some much needed exposure to a larger demographic, and as Myseron explains, "Getting some TV will lead to more TV. If we get Worlds, maybe we'll get the USGP. And if we get the USGP, then maybe in New England we'll get the Shimano Series. Once those things start happening, it's real professional sports. We're running a professional sports league." And that's when the shift from a fringe sport to a major American pastime begins to happen.

Katie Compton has the most Euro and US experience out of any other elite racer in the US, and she has high hopes for the future of American cyclocross. That is, if we can work out a few kinks.

"I think just the excitement for it all over the country, and the depth of the women's field is huge. I think it's deeper than it's ever been. I think we're racing faster and I think the courses are getting faster, but to a point where that might be more negative than positive." Compton explains that this is because "there are so many amateurs racing, I think part of the fast growth is that the courses are getting dumbed down enough to make them easy for the beginners so they aren't challenging for the pros and that's starting to become an issue."

That may not initially seem like a bad thing, but Compton explains: "We don't have the skills when we go to Europe to be competitive. But we need the growth, we need the amateurs, that drives our US 'cross market. It's a participant sport. There is an easy way for promoters to change the tape between races so it appeals to the masses and at amateurs who can come out and race a fun race and the pros can race the technical sections and the amateurs have something cool to watch."

Still, she and Johnson share a common thread in their looks at cyclocross's future: broadcasting. "It's going to change spectator-wise, more people will get involved as they can watch races online. People are going to get into it more and people are actually going to have two bikes and six sets of wheels and have all the gear. People will get more involved than they are now."

Kaitie Antonneau may still be a young racer (in ten years, she'll still be under 30), but she's been around long enough to see some changes and witness the growth of the sport. "I think it's growing over here for sure, I think it's not going to happen overnight, but it's growing. Having Worlds here will help us take a step in the right direction. The courses will become more challenging and I think Europe will respect us more for having cyclocross here and it growing. We want to be successful and embrace it, and I know it's not 'our' sport because they say cyclocross is a Euro sport, but we want to embrace that culture, too, and have it be a big sport over here, too. And hopefully in ten years, that will happen."

However, even young racers know enough to be cautious about too much, too fast. Luke Keough is the first to say that, "It could get big if they don't try to grow it too fast." He isn't so sure that the European model could ever be sustainable in the US, and for good reason: "There's a fine line between races that you have to pay to watch or just getting people out there. I think we need to focus on getting the crowds there first, then maybe it can be self-sustained like it is in Europe. It's more of an event there than it is in the US but we're getting there. And if nothing else, I think more people are going to get into it just because it's fun."

At the pro level, races do need to grow from where they are now if elite racers are to be competitive in Europe, and one thing that promoters and racers alike have mentioned is the need to develop a showcase series in the US that is devoted strictly to elite-level races and courses that equal those in Europe. "I think we're going to have to develop some showcase events. I think you'll see a lot more CrossVegas type things that are elite level races," Richard Fries says. "The day is just getting too crowded and that's OK, but I think we'll see some showcase things happen that will be awesome."

With the changes in technology starting to change the classic cyclocross bike into something that more resembles a mountain bike, with disc brakes, wider tires, and better, faster models coming out every year. "I think there will be a lot of changes in technology and that's already happening. Being able to ride harder and faster and stronger with disc brakes coming and that's just the beginning," Nicole Duke says, "The races are going to get even better because there will be higher standards."

But when you start adding disc brakes to cyclocross bikes, what comes next? As cyclocross bikes get more and more complicated, the fear is that soon, the sport will be turned into a cross-country mountain bike event, for better or worse. Promoter Murphy Mack things cyclocross is growing, "without a doubt." He adds, "We've seen an undeniable surge in numbers here in northern California and I've seen my own team (Superpro Racing) grow from 20 to 60 racers in just five years."

However, Mack predicts a future that for some "purist cyclocrossers" will be far from ideal. "The future I see has a lot of crossover events. The boundaries between the different disciplines are going to become much less defined and much blurrier. You're going to be seeing a lot of mixed terrain races that will pull in riders from MTB, CX and road into the same event." Disc brakes might be just the beginning of the process that blurs the lines between disciplines, which leads to an entirely different set of pros and cons. After all, cyclocross is a unique form of cycling in and of itself, and to begin to hybridize it might be a step backwards: today, we talk about the old days of cyclocross when you raced on a mountain bike because that's what you had. Are we moving towards a day where you race cyclocross on a mountain bike because that's what the pros are doing? With no clear-cut definition for precisely what cyclocross is, how can we preserve it as its own form of racing?

The other question that hovers around cyclocross in the US is, 'will cyclocross in the US ever be held in the same esteem that it is in Europe?' Even the pros don't seem to want it to become the same, despite the larger paychecks that would most likely come with the change.

And perhaps it doesn't need to be. "I think some changes are coming, and I think US racers will be more competitive on the Euro level," Nicole Duke says, "and I think we might see separate sections in courses for the pros versus the amateurs, and with that happening, I think it'll become so much more exciting for spectators."

The idea of bringing the European model to the US doesn't seem to outwardly appeal to anyone, perhaps least of all USA Cycling, since they make their money in race fees not just from elites, but from amateur participants. "I think we'll stick with our participant base," Gullickson says. "It's just a different culture over here. Cycling isn't quite as embedded in the Average Joe's mind as it is in Europe, so you're not going to get the guys who are just fat and smoking and into watching cyclocross. In the US, it's active people who want to be out there and smashing themselves and I think that's the better way in the end." Veteran racer Mark McCormack has seen 'cross through the years, and in his opinion, we need to focus on finding ourselves, not trying to be like Europe. "I am a fan of seeing US 'cross be US 'cross. Let the US stars focus on racing in the US and create its own brand and fan base. We have a great scene here with really good racing. Sure it isn't nearly as fast as Euro 'cross but that doesn't matter. When all the best US guys show up and race together it is a fantastic event with amazing entertainment value."

And at the very top end of the pro spectrum, even the elite-of-the-elite agree with Gullickson's assessment. Tim Johnson argues, "I don't think that what Europe has is a sustainable model that addresses what 'cross is in America. 'Cross is so participant-heavy in a good way. The people are out there doing it on their own. 'Cross in Europe is such a sharp peak and there are only a few people standing on it right now." In the US, he says, we have the numbers: "But we have just a massive space, so as long as our group stays numerous and we do a better job of channeling that passion into successful projects, whether it's TV or books or other promotion of our sport, we'll be successful. I think if we end up with a sharp peak, we're going to end up missing out on a lot of great things. We have a real special thing, and we have a different brand. It's whether or not we can make this brand successful, and what our measure of success is, and we haven't found that yet."

But at the end of the day, Johnson notes, "We're still in flux and that's all right."

PROS DO SOME PREDICTING

"It is such a fun sport and great for spectators. I hope the season remains compressed and continues to gain momentum. I hope we see the main races continue to grow in stature and importance. Right now we have tons of UCI races but not many "big" races. I would like to see every USGP have as many spectators and carry the importance of the National Championships. I also hope we will have TV coverage in 10 years and I can tune in on the weekends and watch it live the way we can now with every major European road race. 10 years ago we could barely catch the Tour de France on TV and now it's on every day for multiple hours in HD. There is no reason we can't get there with cyclocross."   –Todd Wells

"It's not an Olympic sport so it can't get much bigger at the Elite level. We're kind of already there. If anything, we already have decent infrastructure in Europe and we have top riders on foreign teams, like Katie Compton on Rabobank. What does growth mean? Does it mean we see guys like Trebon or Powers ending up on Euro 'cross teams? That's success in road racing, but for the US riders, I don't know about that in 'cross, it's not the pinnacle of it. I think Europe has always looked at the US and thought, 'Oh, that's kind of cool, what they're doing,' but more and more, especially the last two seasons with Bart Wellens coming over and real Euro talent coming over and racing and winning and losing, they're realizing, 'You guys are kind of doing it for real over there,' and they see how good our scene is and how fun our scene is."

–Molly Cameron

"It's going to be a big year. People are worried we're going to go the same way as mountain biking, where we get too big for our britches and collapse under the weight, we're going to start charging $100 entry fees, and it's a fad, and it's going to end. And I just don't see it."

–Adam Myerson

GLOSSARY

Barriers: wooden hurdles set out on a cyclocross course as obstacles, typically not higher than 40 centimeters

Category 1/2/3/4: (also Cat. 1/2/3/4) a rider's designation. A Cat 4 is typically a beginner, while a Cat 1 or Pro is an elite racer. To upgrade to the next category, a racer needs to earn upgrade points by placing well in races.

Cyclocross: (also CX, 'cross, cyclo-cross) a form of bike racing similar to a hybrid of road and mountain bike racing. See Chapter 1 for a full explanation

Palmares: list of accomplishments in sport

Series: a selection of races that are scored together for an overall winner in various categories

Tubular: a type of tire with the tube built in, as opposed to the standard clincher tire that has a separate tube inside of it.

USA Cycling: the governing body of cycling in the US

USGP: United States Gran Prix of Cyclocross

UCI: Union Cycliste Internationale, the governing body of cycling in the world

UCI RACE LOCATIONS

NATIONALS RESULTS
1963-2012

YEAR	LOCATION	GOLD	SILVER	BRONZE
2012	Madison, Wisconsin	Jeremy Powers	Ryan Trebon	Jonathan Page
2010	Bend, Oregon	Todd Wells (3)	Ryan Trebon	Jeremy Powers
2009	Bend, Oregon	Tim Johnson (3)	Ryan Trebon	Jonathan Page
2008	Kansas City, Missouri	Ryan Trebon (2)	James Driscoll	Jonathan Page
2007	Kansas City, Kansas	Tim Johnson (2)	Jonathan Page	Todd Wells
2006	Providence, Rhode Island	Ryan Trebon	Jonathan Page	Tim Johnson
2005	Providence, Rhode Island	Todd Wells (2)	Ryan Trebon	Jonathan Page
2004	Portland, Oregon	Jonathan Page (3)	Ryan Trebon	Todd Wells
2003	Portland, Oregon	Jonathan Page (2)	Todd Wells	Ryan Trebon
2002	Napa, California	Jonathan Page	Todd Wells	Travis Brown
2001	Baltimore, Maryland	Todd Wells	Tim Johnson	Marc Gullickson
2000	Overland Park, Kansas	Tim Johnson	Mark Gullickson	Mark McCormack
1999	San Francisco, California (Presidio)	Mark Gullickson	Bart Bowen	Tim Johnson

Year	Location	1st	2nd	3rd
1998	Fort Devens, Massachusetts	Frank McCormack (2)	Steve Larsen	Jonathan Page
1997	Lakewood, Colorado	Mark McCormack		
1996	Seattle, Washington	Frank McCormack	Mark McCormack	Jan Wiejak
1995	Leicester, Massachusetts	Jan Wiejack (2)	Mark McCormack	Daryl Price
1994	Seattle, Washington	Jan Wiejack	Don Myrah	Dale Knapp
1993	Sonora, California	Don Myrah (4)	Pete Webber	
1992	Golden, Colorado	Mark Howe	Don Myrah	Steve Tilford
1991	Waltham, Massachusetts	Don Myrah (3)	Mark McCormack	
1990	Bremerton, Washington	Don Myrah (2)	Larry Hibbard	Laurence Malone
1989	Milwaukee, Wisconsin	Don Myrah	Jan Wiejak	Paul Curley
1988		Casey Kunselman	Don Myrah	
1987	Bremerton, Washington	Clark Natwick (4)	Don Myrah	Paul Curley
1986	Scotts Valley, California	Clark Natwick (3)		
1985	Nutley, New Jersey	Paul Curley		
1984		Steve Tilford (2)		
1983	Plymouth MA	Steve Tilford		
1982		Clark Natwick (2)		
1981	Pacifica, California	Clark Natwick (1)	Myron Lind	Joe Ryan

1980	Colorado Springs, Colorado	Joe Ryan	Mark Jansen	Davis Phinney
1979	Eugene, Oregon	Laurence Malone (5)	Joe Ryan	Clark Natwick
1978	Austin, Texas	Laurence Malone (4)	Clark Natwick	John Howard
1977	Milwaukee, Wisconsin	Laurence Malone (3)	Clark Natwick	Joe Ryan
1976	Sunriver, Oregon	Laurence Malone (2)	Joe Ryan	Mark Pringle
1975	Berkeley, California	Laurence Malone	Dan Nall	Joe Ryan
1970-74	NOT HELD			
1969	Palos Park, Illinois	John Howard		
1968	Florissant, Missouri	Mike Carnahan		
1967	Florissant, Missouri	Leroy "Tyger" Johnson (3)		
1966	Palos Park, Illinois	Leroy "Tyger" Johnson (2)		
1965	Palos Park, Illinois	Herman Kron (2)		
1964	Palos Park, Illinois	Herman Kron		
1963	Palos Park, Illinois	Leroy "Tyger" Johnson		

MOLLY HURFORD is an editor for *Cyclocross Magazine*, where she writes about every aspect of the sport, from race reports to mechanical how-tos. She also writes a column about her racing experiences, called The Girl With the Cowbell Tattoo. A Mid-Atlantic racer by birth, she now lives in one of the major hubs of New England cycling. When not writing for *Cyclocross Magazine* or The Embrocation Cycling Journal, she's probably out riding her bike, or talking about it. Molly is also a USA Cycling Level 3 coach, and races cyclocross, road and mountain bikes, with the occasional (less publicized) triathlon thrown into the mix.

CPSIA information can be obtained at www.ICGtesting.com
Printed in the USA
LVOW10s1903081014

407873LV00001B/234/P